VOLUME

2

REAL ESTATE TITLE SEARCH

Abstracting

Copyright © 2011 Hennin
ISBN-13: 978-1-933039-64-0

Library of Congress -in-Publication Data
October 04
Txu-1-204-543
Real Estate Title Search
Abstracting

10 9 8 7 6 5 4 3 2 1

The enclosed material is designed for educational purposes only. Each State may have different certification and specific guidelines. Please refer to your State for additional and future information. The information contained herein is considered correct at the time of creation but laws and regulations are updated frequently and the reader assumes the responsibility for confirming current regulations and applicable data. The publisher and author make no warranty as to the success of the individuals using the training material contained herein. The publisher and author make no warranty as to any action taken by any individual completing this program. The reader is responsible for the appropriate use of the materials and information provided. This publication is designed to provide accurate and authoritative information concerning the subject matter. All material is sold with the understanding that neither the author nor the publisher guarantees the actions of any individual making use of the inclusions. Neither the author nor the publisher is rendering a legal opinion, accounting recommendation or other professional service. If legal advice or other expert assistance is desired, the services of a legal professional or other individual should be sought. The applicable federally released forms, disclosures and notices are generated from public domain. Copyright law does apply to all intellectual materials and all rights under said law are reserved b y the copyright owner.

Coursework is available at special quantity discounts to use as premiums and sales promotions within corporate or private training programs. To obtain information or inquire about availability please write to Director, PO Box 1, Hollidaysburg, PA 16648.

NOTICE

REAL ESTATE TITLE SEARCH

Abstracting

Congratulations on your decision to obtain the knowledge, tools, and skills that you need to become a real estate title abstractor. The art of abstracting is one that involves a variety of skills. To begin the process of competently completing an abstract of title, you must first gain insight into the skills you must have in order to achieve success. These skills include an understanding of the fundamentals of real estate as it applies to the real property title you will research as well as an analysis of the specific tasks of title abstracting. You must also gain insight into the processes that occur beyond the research work that you will complete at the courthouse.

Title abstracting is a core function within the real estate and mortgage lending industries. Many of the transactions that occur are able to do so because of the work that you will complete in reviewing and detailing the public records pertaining to the subject property you are to research.

This coursework will provide you with fundamentals of real estate, the essential elements, and practices of title abstracting, and a look into the advanced practices involved in the issuance of title insurance. Regardless of your goals in the completion of this course, you should review each section carefully to ensure that you gain the fundamental skills that will enable you begin on the path to abstracting success.

A title searcher must have the ability to

- Accurately locate and review public records

- Establish a chain of title

- Determine any defect to the title that may exist

- Document the status of these defects

Advanced abstractor duties incorporate many additional tasks including

- The creation of title commitments

- The underwriting of specific issues on a property

- The issuance of title policies that contain title bulletins and exceptions

These advanced functions will become essential if you proceed up the promotional ladder at a title insurance or closing company. Training in advanced abstractor career options is available. We will lightly touch on some advanced knowledge to assist you in understanding the processes that occur beyond those that you will initially perform. Your goal today, with regard to these advanced functions, should be to gain a basic understanding of what will occur because of your careful abstract of the title. These specific advanced functions will be the responsibility of other individuals on your team and these individuals will rely heavily on the abstract you perform to complete their job functions.

Upon initial review, these highlighted tasks may seem simple, but the reality is that the action of preparing an abstract of title involves intricate and time-consuming processes. Fundamental abstracting skills require that you

- Employ a methodical approach to the completion of the required tasks

- Bring high levels of focus to your work

- Provide careful research of the applicable records to ensure that you define and address all matters evident within the chain

- Strive toward the concise completion of each task that falls within your duties

These characteristics are the ones that most title companies will look for in a job candidate. By keeping these primary characteristics in focus while completing your training and job search processes you will find that securing the position that is correct for you is an exciting and simple process. The last Chapter in this course is devoted to assisting you in honing your skills and capitalizing on your strengths. This chapter will assist you in isolating which of the most effective abstracting characteristics you have already mastered and in determining what areas will require dedicated study to enhance.

The positions available in the title industry are rewarding and secure. You will find the completion of this coursework and honing of your innate talents is well worth the time and effort you will expend in learning the job specific activities.

Once you have completed your fundamental skills coursework, you will have created the solid foundation you will need to begin your career as a professional real estate title abstractor.

- You may obtain full-time employment with a title and closing company gaining the ability to become a part of the fast-paced, exciting world of mortgage finance and closings.

- You may customize your business around your lifestyle. This would be a simple process if you choose to act as a contract employee for a variety of title companies. In this type of position, you allow the companies that need you to bid for your services and you set the hours, the pay structure even the location.

- You may even choose to begin your own business as a private title abstractor. Real estate investors and tax sale attendees will find incredible value in the services you offer through careful abstracting work and concise reports on the property that they desire before they risk their actual purchase money.

Only your imagination and desires limit the opportunities for a knowledgeable, professional abstractor. The first step to opening the doors to these opportunities is building a strong knowledge base that you will transfer to practical use at your local courthouse records room.

One essential item you must understand before you begin the task of gaining your knowledge base is exactly why an abstract of title is so vital to the real estate transfer process.

The goal of each action that you take is to assess the legal rights and limitations attached to a particular property or piece of land. Your position will require you to perform the necessary tasks to trace the chain of title of a particular property from present day into the past. During this tracing activity, you will locate any events that have occurred throughout the chain of title that may affect the rights of the landowner. The primary concern to the abstractor is how any event within the public records system affects the ability of the current property owner to transfer full rights in the property to another individual. Any occurrence that limits the property owner's rights to full enjoyment or use of the property is an issue that you must address.

Course Goals

Throughout this program, you will gain a thorough understanding of exactly what is included in an abstract of title and the steps that you will follow in the completion of the abstract.

An abstract of title is the chronological history of the most relevant parts of every recorded instrument regarding a title.

These items of importance may include deeds, contracts, liens, taxes, judicial proceedings, easements, encumbrances, and any other matter that affects the chain of title of a tract of land.

You will research every activity that affects a specific title from the date of the original government grant to the date that you conduct the research compilation.

Your primary duty as a title abstractor or searcher is to determine the rights and interests in the land and the ability of these rights to transfer from the seller to the buyer.

- The beginning Chapters of this coursework will provide you with an overview of the history of land transfer methods and the most commonly used methods in the United States.

- This segment will define the concepts inherent in the real estate bundle of rights system and the transfer of these estates, rights, and interests.

- The coursework will assist you in gaining a foundation of knowledge regarding real estate descriptions and locations.

  This knowledge will assist you in determining actions that exist regarding a specific piece of land. Your primary focus is any action that limits the new owner's rights in relationship to the use of that land.

- Throughout the following days, you will gain the ability to assess the current titleholder's rights to transfer the real estate.

- The course will then move you through the types of liens you may encounter and the methods you will use to determine the status of these liens.

- You will also review the primary types of contracts and deeds you will find recorded for your research purposes at the courthouse.

  Familiarity with these frequently seen documents will allow you to feel secure in your research abilities.

- The coursework will direct your focus to the public records you will encounter and the systems currently in use across the country to organize and store these records.

The ability to gain access to the records you require in your research in an efficient manner will allow you to focus your valuable time on the documents themselves. It also minimizes the time spent on the frustrating task of locating the information you require.

After you have gained a solid foundation of knowledge of the composition of real estate, the transfer processes, documents you may encounter and the actual methods you will use to locate these documents, you will begin the process of learning how your new career position will integrate into the title commitment and insurance processes.

The title search will obtain the essential information found in the documents of the public records that enable the title insurance company to determine facts pertaining to the real property. It is the function of the abstractor to

- Perform a thorough search through all available records

- Note the salient points of each document pertinent to the property being researched

- Trace the outcome or status of every act that has been taken in the past with regard to the property

The purpose of these activities is to gain the information necessary to make two specific determinations.

1. If the individual representing himself or herself as the owner of the property actually has the legal right to transfer the property in question

2. What if any defects exist on the title of the property being researched including those defects brought against the current or past owner that directly impact the clarity of the title

You will compile the results of this search into a report. In many States, this report will be termed the Abstract of Title. The abstract of title is the compilation of all matters that exist in the record concerning the property. You will report all documents and results that you find within the records, but will not draw conclusions as to the final status, exceptions, or methods of insuring these matters. A senior title company employee will use the inclusions of your report to generate yet another document often termed a preliminary title report, prelim, or commitment of title report. This report will reflect the current condition of the title as reported by the abstract of title and state exceptions or conditions placed upon the insurance of the title by the title insurance company.

In order to trace the chain of title, you, as the abstractor, will search all records located at the offices of the

- County recorder

- County assessor

- Any other government agencies applicable to your region

During this search, you will have four primary determinations or goals in place. You must confirm

1. The exact description and location of the property

2. The current estate or interest in the property

3. The vesting of the estate or interest in the property

4. Any exceptions such as liens, encumbrances, easements, and defects that affect the property

Each document that you must review to compile your report will be located within the public records filed at your county courthouse. You must carefully and accurately review each of these documents and compile all of the inclusions into a clear and concise report. This report serves as the basis for the title commitment.

You will review some or all of the following items or records.

- **Property Location and Description**

  It is vital that you locate the correct property and compare all legal descriptions found with regard to that property with the maps located within the courthouse records. These descriptions and map views will also assist you in locating access, right of way and potential easements or encumbrances currently affecting the property.

  These maps and survey descriptions will contain information pertaining to

  ➢ Easements

  ➢ Right of Ways

  ➢ Property Description

  ➢ Right of Access

  ➢ Abutting or adjoining property and roads

- **Assessor's Records**

  The assessor's records will contain information regarding real estate property taxes, special assessments, and the status of payment of these assessments and any tax liens or judgments that exist against the property. When reviewing the assessor's records you will gain information regarding

> ➤ Current property taxes

> ➤ Delinquent Taxes

> ➤ Special Assessments

> ➤ Tax Liens

- **Chain of Title**

The chain of title will include every buyer and seller name and every document recorded pertaining to a particular piece of property from the date of the original land grant through the present. You will examine each document found within the records for authenticity, correctness, and the legal status of any inclusion or matter within the document.

Any matter that remains active against the property or that you are unable to prove is no longer applicable will generate an exception on the title commitment.

These items are termed a break in the chain of title or a blemish on the title and the location of these matters is an integral portion of your search function.

- **Grantor-Grantee Index or General Index**

These indexes list all items that pertain to an individual by name. Items included within these indexes that you must research include

> ➤ Real property transfer documents

> ➤ Liens

> ➤ Judgments

> ➤ Assignments

> ➤ Power of attorney

> ➤ Additional Contracts

> ➤ Other matters pertaining to the specific title you are researching

The items included within these indexes pertain to the individual. All items pertaining to the subject of the search will be apparent whether they pertain to a piece of real property or not.

When reviewing these documents it is important to pay close attention to the format of the names of the individuals. Many times the name of a particular individual will take many formats.

Example: John Doe

Jonathan Doe

John A Doe

Jonathan A Doe

These name formats may pertain to one individual or may actually refer to four different individuals. It is essential that the abstractor note any discrepancies in names used during recordation. The final commitment will contain inclusions or exceptions pertaining to these name formats.

- **General Execution Docket**

  The general execution docket lists any judgments that appear in the record. These judgments might include notes, suits for money damages, breach of contracts actions, unpaid accounts, or any matter for which a there is a judgment for a money damage award.

  You must determine the status of these judgments as well as the specific property, if any, against which these judgment liens exist.

- **Lis Pendens Index**

  The Lis Pendens index shows any pending suits that exist in record that might affect the clarity of the title you are researching.

  You should review these dockets to determine if an owner of record to the property you are researching appears in any pending action or lawsuit.

The following chapters will assist you in gaining the necessary knowledge base and skill group you will need to complete each of the four essential tasks required to create an abstract of title. Each section details the type of records you will encounter the methods of research you will employ within these records and the items of inclusion for the completed abstract.

Title companies and insurance commitments base their entire process around the work that you perform during your research. Your functions are an integral part of the flow of these businesses and as such, it is essential that you gain the knowledge necessary to perform the most concise abstract possible. Much of the material covered in this coursework provides you with the background or base knowledge you will need before you ever enter the records systems to search the title on your first piece of real property. Specific companies and statutory law will alter or amend the materials covered in this course. The materials do not provide a legal opinion by the author or publisher. The inclusions serve as an informational guide in building the foundation of your new career. When you your coursework and study is complete and you feel ready to begin searching the public records, we recommend that you take your coursework and notes along with your abstracting worksheets with you to the courthouse. This will enable you to refer to your course materials frequently and ensure that you are performing your activities with complete accuracy.

The career of real estate title abstractor is essential to the operation of the real estate title insurance and closing industries and as such requires careful, detail oriented, and methodical practices on your part.

CHAPTER

1

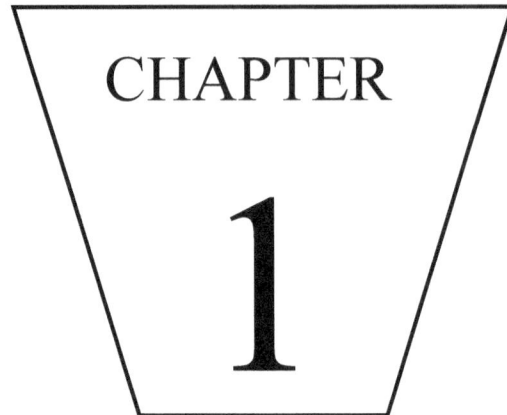

Real Property

UNDERSTANDING REAL PROPERTY INCLUSIONS

One of the most vital keys to the successful completion of an abstract of title is the knowledge of the nature and description of real property. You must obtain a comprehensive understanding of real property so that you are certain you have researched every aspect of the documents filed within the public record system that might limit the ownership interest of the property.

W hen an individual makes a purchase of a piece of property, they are buying more than just a piece of land. The purchase of real property may include the fixtures, improvements, and land as well as specific rights as to the uses of aspects of the land. The items included with the purchase of real property are referred to as the bundle of rights and you must understand what portion of this bundle is being transferred with each document that you research within the public records system.

- You must gain a comprehensive understanding of the term real property.

- You should cultivate the ability to review deeds and other records to determine what inclusions or limitations might effect the transaction for which you are conducting the research.

When you have gained all of the base knowledge incorporated into this course, you will be able to feel secure that you are conducting the most complete abstract of title possible.

The following sections will provide you with a comprehensive understanding of what is included in real property transactions as well as the possible methods that may have been employed in the dividing of the rights to the portions of the real property.

REAL PROPERTY Real property includes the land. A parcel of land carries with it additional rights that you must research. The three basic rights included within the transfer of land are surface, air and sub-surface rights.

Surface rights Surface rights include anything that is on the land, or permanently attached to the land and can be numerous. You must scrutinize these rights during your research, as they are the most common restrictions you will encounter. The following segment will define the surface rights, common restrictions to these rights, and the affect any restriction within the records you are restrictions will have on your abstracting report.

Sub-surface rights Sub-surface rights include anything that is below the land such as coal, water, ore, mineral deposits, etc.

Sub-surface rights are typically included in the bundle of rights during a real estate transfer.

Subsurface rights include the rights to the space and natural resources that are contained to beneath the surface of the earth of the property.

The term sub-surface right is defined as the right to all or certain specific natural resources that lie beneath a parcel of land.

Sub-surface rights typically include the right to enter beneath the surface of the land explore the area beneath the surface of the land for natural resources and extract the natural resources from the land .

Mineral rights are an example of an inclusion within the term subsurface rights.

Sub-surface resources are subject to the same rights of ownership as any other portion of the land.

> The right of ownership to these resources may be severed from the overall bundle of rights.

> A portion of your research function will be to make a determination as to whether the sub-surface rights have been severed from the overall bundle of rights.

It is important that you make adequate inquiry into the public records to determine what rights are intact with regard to the property you are researching. The severance of a resource right may be completed through a variety of methods and it is important that you review any document that pertains to the bundle of rights. You should review the records pertaining to the property you are researching paying specific attention to

- Conveyance or grant document

- A lease of the named rights

- A mortgage against the minerals

- Adverse possession

- A contract between parties that pertains specifically to the resources

- A judicial determination

If any of the documents listed above or additional documents pertaining to the severance of rights are in existence concerning the property you are researching, it is vital that you fully review each document. You must determine the status and transferability of these specific rights.

Sub-surface right severance allows different owners to hold title to different resources that belong to the same parcel of land. In addition, the severance of resource rights may affect the rights of ownership for the property you are researching.

You must note any severance of sub-surface rights within your abstracting report. The title insurance company will wish to review any severance of sub-surface rights to make a determination as to how to address the item within the Title Insurance Commitment.

Air Rights

Air rights include anything that is directly above a particular parcel of land such as electrical wires, tree limbs and in most cases the actual section of air and atmosphere.

Generally, the rights to the ownership of a piece of land also include the rights to occupy and use the airspace above the surface of the land.

In real estate law, airspace is defined as a unit of real estate three-dimensionally described (L, W, H) created through the horizontal subdivision of the space existing over a particular tract of land.

It is important to remember that airspace is subject to conveyance and other forms of alienation the same as any other right included with the bundle of rights. Air rights are also subject to any matter, lien, or encumbrance that affects the land.

Possible transfers of airspace would include the sale of condominiums, walkways, and navigational easements.

> The transfer of air rights consists of any right granted to another to use the space above the surface of a particular parcel or piece of land.

A unit of airspace is known as an air lot. The identification of an air lot includes the parcel of land beneath the unit and the addition of the horizontal and vertical parameters of the unit or lot.

Airspace ownership is subject to

o   Federal regulations

o   Statutory provisions

o   Local government disposition

o   Zoning ordinances

o   Private or individual restrictions or limitations

These restrictions and limitations are commonly found in the areas of navigable space, airwaves etc.

Real estate transactions that involve airspace and air rights are extremely complex. You should carefully review any document that indicates a severance of air rights that you discover during your research. You should copy any document that refers to the severance of air rights in its entirety and attach it as an addendum to your abstracting report. The title insurance underwriter will wish to review the applicable documents before making a title commitment on the property.

Understanding the method of land parcel ownership is a vital key in the understanding of the air rights, surface rights, and sub-surface rights of a piece of property.

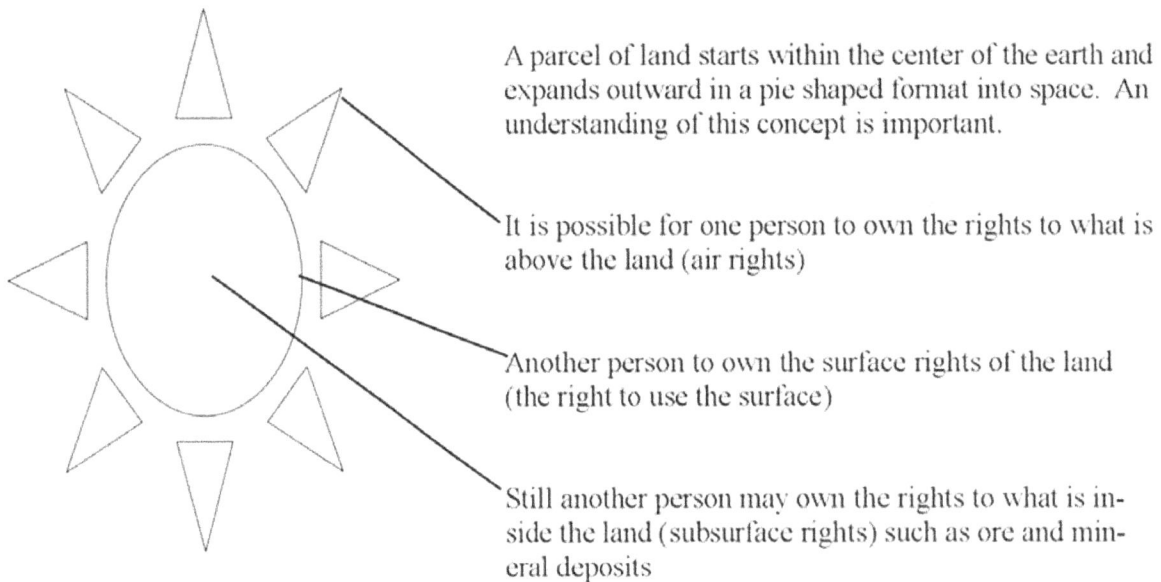

A parcel of land starts within the center of the earth and expands outward in a pie shaped format into space. An understanding of this concept is important.

It is possible for one person to own the rights to what is above the land (air rights)

Another person to own the surface rights of the land (the right to use the surface)

Still another person may own the rights to what is inside the land (subsurface rights) such as ore and mineral deposits

Figure 1:1 Diagram Real Property Rights

Surface Rights

Surface rights are the rights to the land and the improvements of the land.

Real Property surface rights include the improvements that exist that are actually affixed to the surface of the land.

IMPROVEMENTS The term real property includes improvements. Improvements include anything affixed to the surface of the land.

- Buildings, structures, pipeline, pavement, fences, etc

- An item of personal property that has been attached to the land might then become a real property

  Personal property affixed to the land in such a way that it is considered a real property improvement then becomes known as a fixture

- Trees, perennials, and vegetation on the land are also a part of real property. These are known as fruits of nature.

- Anything else affixed to the land that improves the value of the land is a part of real property.

Ownership of real property also includes the rights to use the land and improvements. The land may contain improvements that also fall under the term real property.

When a seller is selling a piece of real property, he or she is actually selling the rights to use all of the items that are a part of that property.

Any reference to the severance of a surface right, a lien on an item that is considered a surface right or other matter dictating an unusual circumstance pertaining to the surface rights of a parcel of land should be carefully scrutinized. You should make a determination as to what actions the document implies, the status of these actions, and make a copy of the applicable document for inclusion as an addendum to your abstracting report.

FIXTURES The items within the home that are categorized as fixtures are typically included in a transfer transaction. Fixtures would fall under the category of surface rights.

A fixture is a piece of personal property that has been affixed, installed, or permanently attached to a parcel of land or the structures on the land.

If the piece of personal property is permanently attached according to the lawful description, the item then becomes a part of the real estate.

You can apply four standards to determine if an item is a fixture.

1.   The intention of the parties in the transaction

2.   An agreement between the parties in the transaction concerning the status of the particular item in question

3.   The manner in which the item is attached to the real property

4.   The item itself and its adaptation to the real estate

In some states, liens placed upon fixtures are recorded in a specific manner that allows for the premise that any purchaser or mortgagor of the property has notice of the lien. This constructive notice would prohibit the underwriting of this fixture and its full, essential transfer despite the meeting of the four qualifications listed above.

Example: A built in appliance for which on outside company has provided financing could be a secured item.

The appliance acts as security against the funds provided for the purchase of the appliance.

The appliance would then be subject to a lien outside of the standard liens typically encountered in a real estate transaction.

When a particular fixture is secured in this manner, an exception must be noted in Schedule B of the Title Commitment removing the insurance coverage to this particular piece or item.

You should copy any document pertaining to the fixture in its entirety and include it as an addendum to the abstracting report.

If you do not discover notice of the lien during the search process, title insurance policies generally insure good title to fixtures that are affixed to the property in a manner that causes them to be construed as real property.

PERSONAL PROPERTY

If an item is classified as personal property, it will not be included in the sale of real property. Items that may fall under this category include:

- Detached furniture and appliances

- Business articles affixed to a rented building by a tenant

- Annual cultivated plants and crops are known as fructus industrias (Fruits of Industry) or emblements.

CROPS: It is common for the sale of plants and crops to fall within the sale of land. A transaction conveying land that contains crops typically includes the crops grown or to be grown on the land.

In some cases, crops may be sold by contract apart from the land. If the crops are not to be included in the transaction, they must be specifically excepted in Schedule B of the title commitment and policy.

If you locate a specific contract negotiating the sale of crops outside of the transaction for which you are completing the research, you must generate a notice on your abstract report and include a copy of the entire document as an addendum to your abstracting report. This allows the underwriter to be aware of the terms of this contract and to create the applicable exception.

```
    ┌─────────────────────────┐
    │      CHAPTER            │
    │                         │
    │         2               │
    └─────────────────────────┘
```

Land Location and Description

Land descriptions will take a variety of forms and each will be used during your abstracting process. Each method of description carries with it certain advantages and disadvantages and the document you are reviewing will use the descriptive method that is most advantageous in relationship to that particular document. Therefore, the descriptive reference used will depend on the document you are reviewing. It is important that you understand how the different methods relate to each other and are able to apply each reference to the property being researched. A comprehensive knowledge of the various location descriptions will enable you to move between documents that use different descriptive methods with confidence that you are researching the correct parcel of land.

L and is described using a variety of methodology. Each method refers to the same parcel. The ability to review various methods of reference and confirm the location of the property you are researching using each method is essential to the proper compilation of your abstracting report.

1. INFORMAL REFERENCE

Informal reference is the description of land by the street numbers and place names.

Example: 123 Realty Street

The advantage of the informal reference method is that it is easily understood.

The disadvantage of the informal reference method of describing land that it is not a precise location that is easily confirmed as the parcel you are attempting to locate. Street names and numbers describing a parcel are often similar to those describing another parcel and can be confused. The informal reference does not provide exact boundaries of the land and the numbers and names of the streets used in informal reference tend to change over the years making it an unreliable descriptive method.

It is often best to reference more than one descriptive method to ensure that you have correctly identified the property being researched.

2. METES AND BOUNDS

The second method of land description is the metes and bounds method. The metes and bounds description is a more exact method of describing the location, form and boundary of real estate.

Monument   The metes and bounds description method uses a permanent, man-made monument or reliable fixed location as a beginning point for the description.

This monument is set at one corner of the parcel and is typically an iron pin or pipe that is driven several feet into the ground. At times, a concrete or stone monument is used. To guard against the possibility that the monument might later be removed, it is referenced by means of a connection line to a nearby permanent reference mark established by a government survey agency.

**Reference
Mark**   Other parcels near the one being described will also be referenced to the same permanent reference mark.

This permanent reference mark allows for easy re-structure of the beginning point for the metes and bounds measurements regardless of the passage of time or the alteration of the post or pin location.

You will see the metes and bounds method of description in many older deeds you encounter during your research. It is important that you learn to construct a specific drawing based on the description so that you can locate understand the exact boundaries of the property you are researching.

Distance and Direction

After affixing the post or pin to a corner of the property, the surveyor then describes the parcel in terms of distance and direction from that point.

The metes and bounds method actually translates as

- distance (metes) and direction (bounds)

- The direction + the distance = the side

The distances in the description are usually expressed in feet but any linear measurement may be used for descriptive purposes. Other linear measurements that may be seen are yards, miles, perches, and rods.

- Direction is shown in degrees, minutes, and seconds

  - 360 degrees in a circle

  - 60 minutes in each degree

  - 60 seconds in each minute

- To obtain the directions to include in the components you would determine the primary direction to be used.

  The primary direction is either north or south.

- Next, you take the degrees of deviation from the primary direction.

  The degree of deviation will not exceed 90 degrees.

  The degree of deviation will deviate from the primary direction toward one of the two secondary directions.

- The secondary directions are east and west.

With the metes and bounds system you would start from the permanent reference mark and use the direction and distance to travel to the nearest corner of the property.

- This is the point where the parcel survey begins and it is known as the point of beginning or point of commencement.

- From this point, you would travel clockwise along the parcel perimeter. Although it is possible to describe a parcel by either going clockwise or counter clockwise, it is customary to go clockwise.

At times, the survey will be so old or the land so changed that it is difficult to locate the survey pin on the actual property or determine the specific boundary lines of the property through another form of description source. When compiling an abstract report it is recommended that you locate at least two different land descriptions for inclusion in the report.

Diagramming Quick list:

1.   Locate the Point of Beginning

2.   Identify the Direction from the Point of Beginning

3.   Identify the Distance to the next point

4.   Repeat the steps until you have outlined 4 sides

Example: Begin at the point on the Western side of 1st Avenue and at the intersection of lots 3 & 4 of the plot plan.

Proceed along the northerly side of lot 3 SOUTH 60 degrees WEST 120 feet to an alley.

Along the EASTERN side of the ally proceed NORTH 59 degrees WEST 60 feet.

Thence continue NORTH 60 degrees EAST 120 feet thence along the same line.

Continue SOUTH 58 degrees EAST 59.6 feet to the place of beginning.

Diagramming Directions

1. North 45 Degrees West   2. South 15 Degrees East

Figure 2:1 Diagramming Directions

3.   RECTANGULAR SURVEY

Another method of land description is the rectangular survey system. This method is sometimes alternately termed a government survey or US public land survey.

The rectangular survey system is designed to provide faster and simpler methods of describing land than the metes and bounds method. Rather than using available physical monuments, the rectangular survey system is based upon imaginary lines.

- These lines are the east-west latitude lines and the north-south longitude lines that encircle the globe.

In terms of landmass, more land in the United States is described using this rectangular survey method than by any other method. If you are reviewing the actual number of property or parcels documented the recorded plat is used more frequently.

It is important that you learn to

- Understand how to read this type of description.

- Compare the recorded description against the property you are searching.

- Be able to locate the property on the plot maps from the description.

Principal Meridians	Principal Meridians is the first item to understand in the rectangular survey method.
	Certain longitude lines are selected as principal meridians and it is upon these lines that the remaining lines are calculated.
Base Line	For each principal meridian there is an intercepting latitude line called a base line.
Correctional Lines	Every 24 miles north and south of a base line are correction lines or standard parallels.
Guidelines	Every 24 miles east and west of the principal meridian, guidelines run from one standard parallel to the next.

These lines are necessary because the earth is a sphere. As one travels north or south, the longitude lines come closer together until they eventually meet at the farthermost north and south points of the globe.

Each set of standard parallels and guide meridians outline a section, which contains 24 mile by 24-mile area. These areas outlined are called a check or quadrangle.

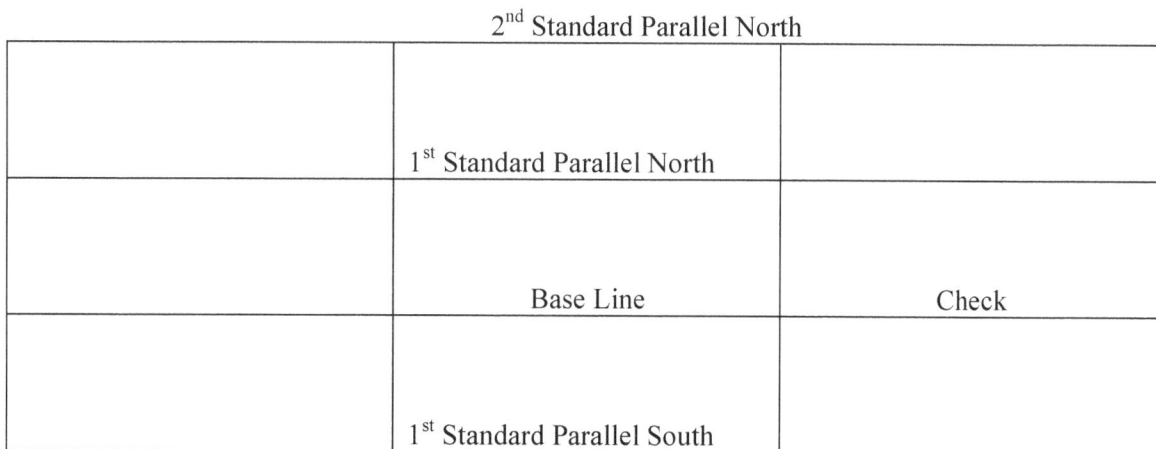

2nd Standard Parallel North

	1st Standard Parallel North	
	Base Line	Check
	1st Standard Parallel South	

Figure 2:2 Diagram 1 – Rectangular Survey

Selected Longitude and Latitude lines serve as Base Lines and Meridians
Each set of standard parallels and guide meridians outline a section that contains a 24 mile by 24-mile area.

The areas outlined are called a check or quadrangle.

There are 36 principal meridians and the intersecting base lines in the US public land survey system.

Every six miles east and west of a principal meridian, imaginary lines are drawn.

This creates 6-mile wide columns, which are then called ranges.

These ranges are numbered consecutively east and west of the meridian.

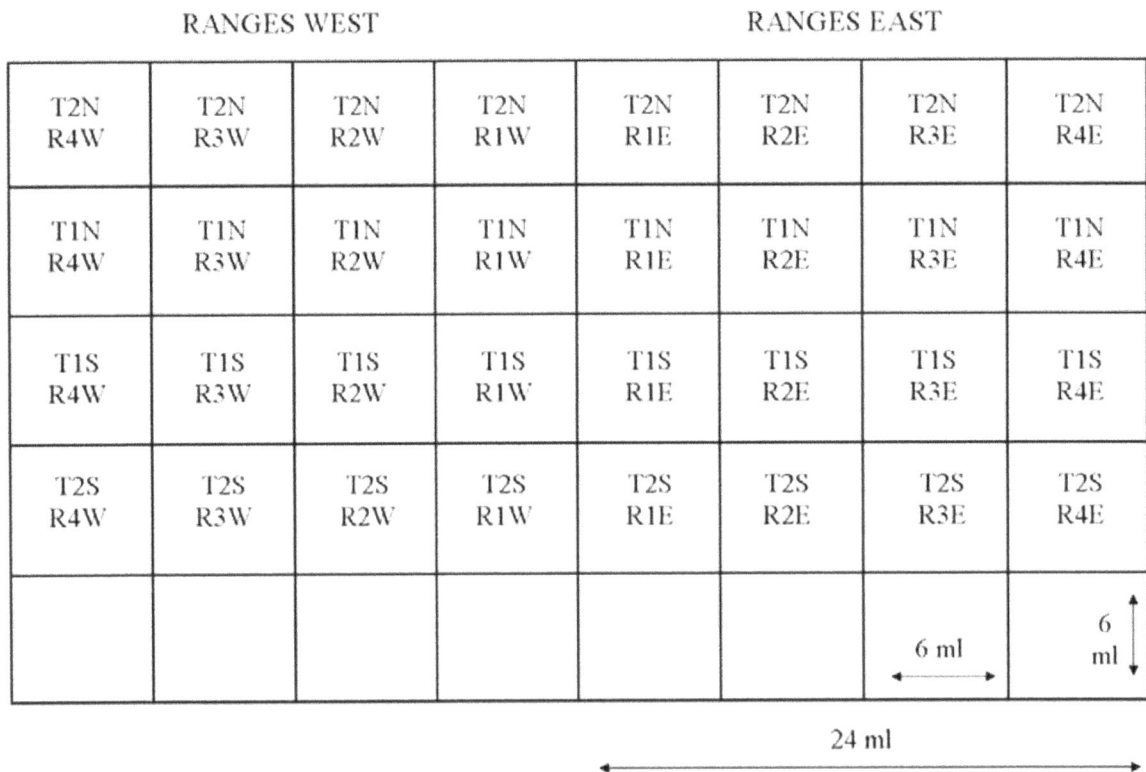

RANGES WEST   RANGES EAST

T2N R4W	T2N R3W	T2N R2W	T2N R1W	T2N R1E	T2N R2E	T2N R3E	T2N R4E
T1N R4W	T1N R3W	T1N R2W	T1N R1W	T1N R1E	T1N R2E	T1N R3E	T1N R4E
T1S R4W	T1S R3W	T1S R2W	T1S R1W	T1S R1E	T1S R2E	T1S R3E	T1S R4E
T2S R4W	T2S R3W	T2S R2W	T2S R1W	T2S R1E	T2S R2E	T2S R3E	T2S R4E
						6 ml	6 ml

24 ml

Figure 2:3 – Diagram 2 – Rectangular Survey

In turn, every six miles north and south of the base lines another line is drawn.

These lines are known as township lines.

These township lines are then numbered in a similar manner to the ranges with the numbers increasing as you move away from the line.

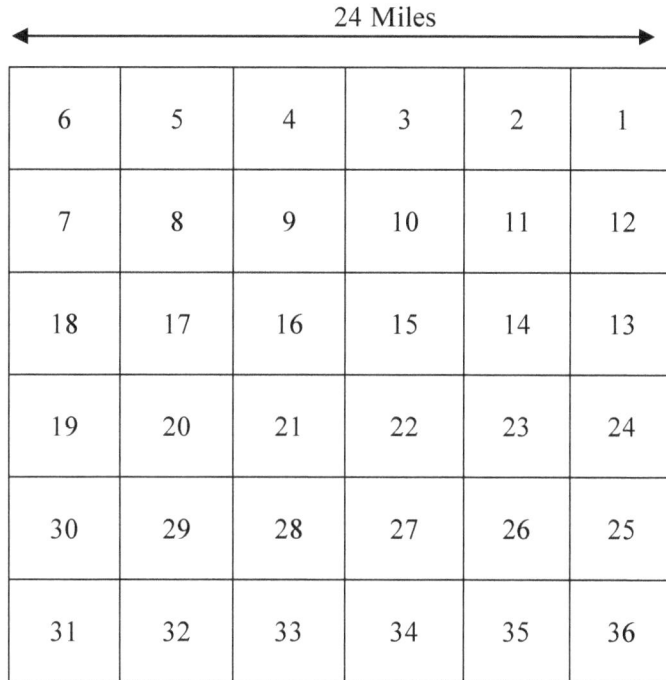

24 Miles					
6	5	4	3	2	1
7	8	9	10	11	12
18	17	16	15	14	13
19	20	21	22	23	24
30	29	28	27	26	25
31	32	33	34	35	36

Figure 2:4 Diagram 3 – Rectangular Survey

Each of these imaginary boxes created by the ranges and township lines measures 36 square miles.

These imaginary boxes are commonly called townships.

Each of these townships is divided into a 1 square mile portion termed a section. Sections are numbered 1 to 36 beginning in the upper right hand corner of the township and continuing left to right until the sections have all been numbered. In this method, any sections numbered consecutively share a common boundary.

Each 1 square mile section contains 640 acres.

Each acre contains 43,650 square feet. Any parcel of land smaller than a 640-acre section is identified by its position within the section. To do this each section is divided into quarters and halves. This division allows parcels, which are smaller than 640 acres to be identified.

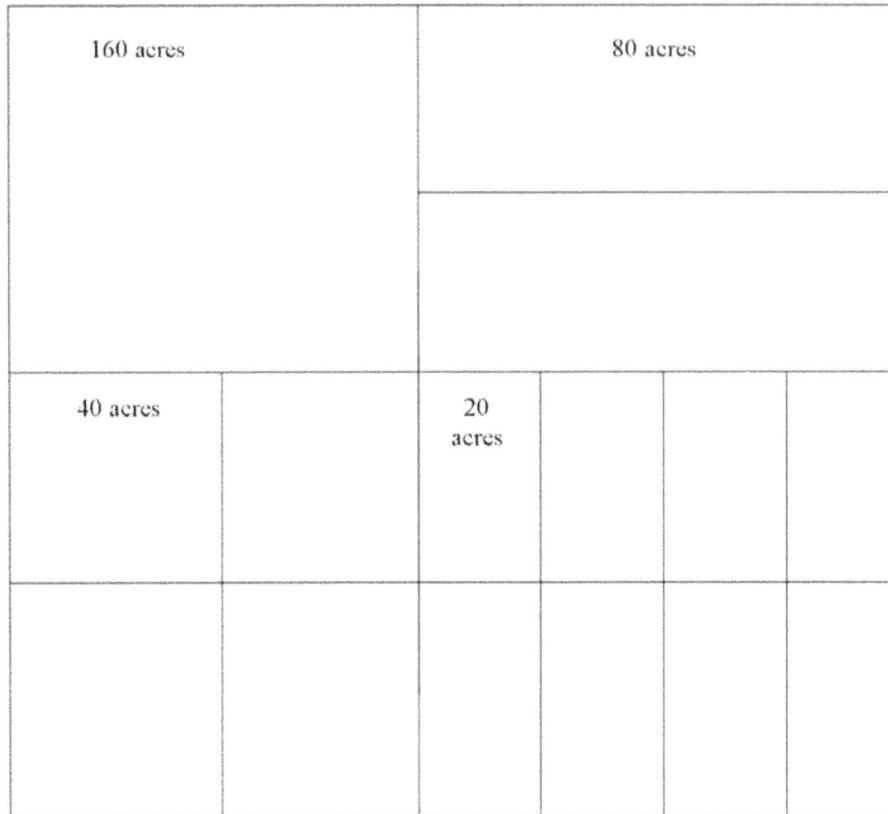

160 acres		80 acres			
40 acres		20 acres			

Figure 2:5 Diagram 4 – Rectangular Survey

Any parcel of land smaller than a 640-acre section is identified by its position within the section.

To do this each section is divided into quarters and halves. This division allows parcels, which are smaller than 640 acres to be identified.

Dividing a section into a quarter creates 160 acres.

Dividing a quarter section by quarters creates 40-acre parcels and so on.

If you are attempting to locate or sketch a rectangular survey, it may be helpful to start at the end or smallest section in the description and work your way outwards.

Some sections using this method will be smaller than the 640 acres. This is because the longitude lines of the earth converge as they near the North Pole. For this reason, not all townships will contain 36 square miles.

4.   RECORDED PLAT

Another method of land description is the Recorded Plat method. This is the simplest and most convenient method of describing land.

- A plat is a map that shows the location and boundaries of individual properties.

- This system is also termed the lot-block-tract system, recorded map, or recorded survey.

This method is used to describe more parcels of land than any other method. In terms of actual landmass, the Rectangular Survey system is used more often but this system is used for more parcels so you should familiarize yourself with the maps and their form.

This method is based on the filing of a surveyor's plat in the public recorder's office. You will encounter this method frequently when you are reviewing courthouse record maps to obtain an exact property location.

- A metes and bounds survey is typically included in the map and then the map is prepared to show the detail boundaries of each parcel.

- Each parcel is then assigned a lot number.

- Each block in the tract will be assigned a block number.

- The tract itself is given a name or number.

These maps are typically placed in a map book or survey book in the county recorder's office. Each plat is assigned a book and page reference number and all of the books are made available to the public in the county recorder's office.

This system is extremely easy to use once you understand the methods of storage.

- Each area that falls under the county jurisdiction will be assigned to a specific book.

- Most map record rooms contain a legend indicating which book you should search for which area of the county.

- Once you have located the correct book, you will open the maps to the correct page as indicated by the parcel map number you are seeking.

- On that page will be each parcel for that particular area. The parcels will be numbered for easy designation.

You will be able to locate the parcel of land you desire by following the series of numbers provided in the description of the property you are researching.

Plat Map with Assessor's Parcel Number

Example 2: 0200-27-19	0200-27-18	Example 1: 0200-27-17	*Example: Lot 1 Assessor Log= 0200-27-17* *Map Book= 200 Map Page= 27 Parcel = 17* *Assessor Log= 0200-27-19*
0200-27-20	0200-27-21	0200-27-17A	*Map Book= 200 Map Page= 27 Parcel = 17*

Figure 2:6 Plat Map with Assessors Parcel Number

Example Explanation: Lot 1

Assessor Log = 0200-27-17
Map Book = 200
The first series of numbers included in the description indicates the map book you should select.
Map Page = 27

The second grouping of numbers shows the page of the map book you must reference.

Parcel   =   17

The last group of numbers indicates the actual parcel you would be purchasing. These numbers are typically assigned in a contiguous manner but at times, the assignment might be complex. This complexity is a result of the continued growth in your area.

Example Explanation: A map number of 17-A would be located in the same manner as is detailed in the previous example.

Locate parcel 17.

Parcel 17 has been subdivided since the original map was created. This sub-division is noted in the map book, but map books are infrequently updated so the notation will be a modification rather than an entire new survey assignment.

You would then locate 17-A. 17-A was once a portion of the parcel designated as 17 and will often be hand-written lines and notations.

5.   ASSESSOR'S PARCEL NUMBER

You may also find reference to the property you are searching in terms of the assessor's parcel number. These are numbers assigned by the tax assessor to aid in the assessment of property for tax collection purposes. Often, the assessor's parcel number and the recorded plat number will be the same in designation.

These parcel numbers are public information and are often used by real estate agents and brokers, appraisers and investors to assist in identifying real property.

The assessor may use a variety of methods to assign these parcel numbers but a common method is to divide the county into map books.

Each of these books is assigned a number. Each book will cover a particular portion of the assessor's county.

Each page of the map book shows specific parcel maps.

Each of these parcel maps will be assigned its own number.

For subdivided lots, these maps will base the numbers on the plats submitted by the sub-divider to the county recorder office when the subdivision was created.

In the case of un-subdivided land, the assessor's office will create its own maps.

Regardless of the source of the maps, the assessor will assign each parcel of land a parcel number.

The assessor's parcel number may or may not be the same as the lot number assigned by the surveyor.

The assessor uses these numbers to produce an assessment roll that lists every parcel in the county assessor's office by parcel number.

These rolls show the current owner's name, address and the assessed value of the land and buildings of that particular property.

These maps are available to the public in the assessor's office. In some instances, a private firm may reproduce the maps and lists and make them available for a fee.

It is important to understand that these maps are not the final authority for the legal description of the property. The legal description of a parcel can only come from a search that includes looking at the current deed to the property and the recorded copy of the sub-divider's plat.

You will often be able to locate the actual property using these maps. When the property you are researching is not subject to any form of issue, this basic location may be sufficient. If an apparent issue such as encroachment exists, then you will want to research further into the records to obtain exact metes and bound style or other exact description to assist you in establishing boundary lines.

6. REFERRAL TO ANOTHER DOCUMENT

Land is also sometimes described by referring to another publicly recorded document.

Example: A deed or mortgage may be referenced to aid in describing a parcel of land.

All that certain lot, parcel, or piece of land described in Deed Book Volume 109, Page 67 at the County of Records.

To be used as reference these documents must contain a full description of the parcel in question. If you encounter a document that only contains a description that references another document, you will need to access this other document in order to obtain the information you require.

7. STATE REFERRAL METHOD

Some states have developed their own, statewide system of reference points for land description and surveying.

Example: In North Carolina, the state is divided into a grid of 84 blocks.

Each side of these blocks corresponds to 30 minutes (1/2 of 1 degree) of latitude or longitude.

This method is called the Grid System and these grid lines intersect at points to which the metes and bounds system can be referenced.

These systems may also be termed coordinate systems and are frequently put into place to help with the surveying of large parcels of land in remote areas.

It is important that you establish the methods of land description used in your State or Jurisdiction. This familiarity will enable you to compare the descriptions in all of the documents you encounter during your search and note any discrepancy that exists

8. SURVEY

A survey is defined as the process of measuring land to determine its exact area.

Surveyors report a map or plat in the form a drawing that shows the exact

- Measurements

- Boundaries

- Areas

- Improvements

- Structures

- Easements

- Utilities

- Features

of a certain parcel of land

Survey requirements are established by each individual state. There are minimum survey standards established by the American Land Title Association and the American Congress of Surveying and Mapping. These standards may be added to or modified by the State in which the survey is conducted.

To be considered valid, a Licensed or Registered Land Surveyor or a Licensed Civil Engineer must complete a survey. State Law may authorize other individuals to conduct surveys within that particular State. If a question arises as to the competence and authority of a specific surveyor, it is best to research the authorization through applicable state agencies before using the survey provided.

The title insurance process will often require that a valid survey be located within the public records system as part of your abstracting services. The ability to incorporate a survey within your report will enable the title underwrite to eliminate certain requirements or exceptions that might otherwise need to be incorporated into the title commitment. These requirements or exceptions are often termed location exceptions.

Reviewing surveys for the purpose of title insurance issuance requires a fine attention to detail. In an effort to confirm that the survey you are reviewing meets the standards of your company, you will wish to review specific items including

- The land record system that was used to develop the survey

- The compliance of the survey and surveyor with the State and General Survey licensure requirements

- The access to and from the property described in the survey

- Whether the legal description included in the survey and on the title and deed match

- Whether the legal description of the property to be purchased matches those descriptions of neighboring properties with no conflict

- Whether those matters affecting the property such as easements, utilities and other items shown on the survey create potential use issues for you after the purchase

Before relying on any single description of land, you should consider the rule regarding a proper legal description. This dictates that you apply a key test to the land description. This test dictates that another person reading the description could go out and locate the piece of land based only upon that description.

APPURTENANCE

In addition to the basic description of the property, the conveyance of land carries with it any appurtenances to the land. An appurtenance is any right, privilege, or improvement that belongs and passes with the land but is not necessarily part of the land.

Example: A common appurtenance would be an easement or right-of-way that given for that particular parcel of land.

You will gain additional details relating to restrictions and appurtenances later in the course. The inclusion of these matters within this area of the course is important because you will often encounter notations regarding these matters during your review of land descriptions.

When reviewing legal descriptions various items may appear and affect the property potential.

QUICK LIST

Accretions	Boundary Line Agreements	Dedicated Areas
Shores	Acreage	Vacated Areas
Lakes	Party Walls	Reservations
Oceans	Roads	Easements
Rivers	Streets	Exceptions
Minerals	Railroads	

In addition to the essential elements such as land mass, measurements, location and form, you should review all applicable land descriptions and maps to determine any additional rights or limitations that the transfer of land may entail.

At times the property may also carry with it additional rights or limitations that may be determined through the scrutiny of the legal description of the property.

You should note any additional right that exists in favor of the property you are researching. These additional rights will be specifically included or excluded from the title commitment and insurance.

You should note the applicable information from any document granting or removing a right that you locate during your research. The following segment details some of the most common rights and interests you will encounter during your research. Additional rights and interests may exist and if you encounter a right or interest not addressed you should consult with the underwriter assigned to the commitment to determine what additional items of research may be required.

Some additional rights are necessary for the use of the property. An example of a necessary right would be the right of access. Without access to the property, the use of that property would be very limited. Other rights might enhance the value of a property. A property that contains Riparian rights would provide the owner of the property the right to use a river or stream located either on or at the border of the property. This could enhance the perceived value of the property.

ACCESS

When examining the property it is important to determine if the property abuts or adjoins another property or a public road or access.

An abutting property is a property where the real estate touches a public road or another piece of real estate.

- If the property abuts a public road, you must determine if the government has issued a conveyance or condemnation relating to direct access to that road.

  The conveyance or condemnation of access could be a serious question when the new property owner attempts to make use of the property. Before the title company for which you are completing the search can issue insurance, they will need an absolute determination as to the right of access granted to the property.

  There are two different types of access.

  Physical Access: Physical access is the actual ability to use an access point to the property. In some instances, a property may abut one or more roads but legally lack the right of access or the use of all of the roads.

  If no legal description defining access these roads exists within the records, the abutment to these roads would be physical access not legal access.

  In other words, the simple existence of a point of access does not necessarily mean that an owner of the property abutting or adjoining the access gains the right to use it. You must conduct further research to ensure that the property you are researching contains legal access points.

Legal Access: Legal access is the legal right to use a described access point to a property.

In most cases, the location of a legal access point for the property you researching will provide the new owner with the ability to gain entry into the property

There will be times that a legal access described in the records does not actually provide a simple method of gaining entry to the property.

A description may exist that defines a right of access by a property to a road that does not yet exist. This right of way may be part of a future development plan. If the legal processes are in place for this creation, the access description may exist within the records you are researching. However, since the right of way or access is planned rather than actual, the property owner may not have the rights to gain entry to the property using that access point until some date in the future. You should note the description of a future legal access and define the present lack of physical access within the abstracting summary.

If the basis of the access to the property you are researching is an established appurtenant easement for ingress and egress, it is important to confirm the validity of the easement. You will incorporate the details illustrating the validity of the easement using the specific terminology within the public records you are researching. You must copy the exact verbiage of the clause for incorporation into the abstracting summary or photocopy the applicable document for inclusion as an addendum to the abstracting summary. The title insurance company issuing the policy for the property may complete an easement review and during issuance. The policy will contain a specific clause relating to "easement insurance".

When researching access you should review some additional considerations. You will describe any findings within the abstracting summary.

QUALITY   You must note the quality of the right of access.

This means that the access might be other than vehicular.

Example: Pedestrian – foot traffic only

Aquatic – via water only

Some other non-conventional form of access.

You should confirm the quality of the access. The quality of the access might affect the title commitment and insurance issuance of the property. You should include the exact verbiage you encounter within the public records into the abstracting summary.

BOUNDARY LINE AGREEMENTS

You may encounter items that reference boundary line issues when you are conducting your research. If there appears to be an issue with the boundary lines of the property, you should review the public records to see if you can locate any reference to an established agreement. Whenever the location of the boundary line division between two properties cannot be accurately determined, specific actions may be required before the transaction for which you are conducting the abstract can be finalized.

1. Schedule B of the title commitment and policy may define an exception to the coverage of the boundary lines of the property.

2. The concerned parties may create and record a valid boundary line agreement.

3. Any party may obtain an accurate to clarify the boundary lines of the property.

   The concerned parties may then create and record of a valid agreement based upon this survey.

4. Any concerned party may obtain a proper judicial pleading and proceeding to obtain a judgment that clarifies the boundary lines.

Any boundary line agreement or issue that you note during your search requires that you copy the exact wording of the matter into the summary. You should obtain copies of all records and survey documents pertaining to the property.

The most common situations that cause boundary line problems are:

> Gaps

> Overlaps

> Imprecise descriptions

- ➢ Improper location of fences

- ➢ Improper location of boundary markers

- ➢ Accreted land

- ➢ Errors in surveys

- ➢ Recorded sub-division maps or land plats

- ➢ Defective legal descriptions

You must treat the possibility of a boundary line dispute very seriously. A title abstractor should never attempt to determine who has the actual right to a portion of land. Any boundary line problems must be solved before the issuance of a title insurance policy. If you discover a potential boundary line issue during your search activity, you should immediately notify the underwriter assigned to the commitment so that the methods that the parties will employ to resolve the issue may be determined.

RIPARIAN RIGHT

The conveyance of a property may include riparian rights. The transfer of ownership of a parcel of land that borders on a river or stream will typically carry with it the right to use that water in common with other landowners whose lands border the same watercourse.

When dealing with Riparian right the landowner does not have absolute ownership of the water that flows past his land but may use it in a reasonable manner.

Some states have modified basic riparian rights through the doctrine of prior appropriation.

- • The doctrine of prior appropriation allows that the first owner who is able to divert water for his own use may continue to do so although it is not equitable to the other owners along the watercourse.

When researching a property that borders a river or stream it is important that you note this border. You must designate an exact description of the land and the areas of the land that border the river or stream. You must also designate any item of record that you locate that either impairs or conveys the riparian rights to the landowner. If no specific record exists with regard to these rights, the underwriter will be aware of the statutes applicable to the property.

LITTORAL RIGHT

Similar to Riparian rights, littoral rights may exist. A parcel that borders a lake or sea carries littoral rights

- Littoral rights allow the landowner to use and enjoy the water touching his land provided he does not alter the position of the water by artificial means.

Ownership of land typically allows the right to drill for water below the surface of that parcel of land.

In some states, a landowner has the right to act in conjunction with the neighboring landowners to draw his share of percolating water.

In other states, limitations to water result from the doctrine of prior appropriation.

- The doctrine of prior appropriation states that the first landowner to divert the water for his use may continue to do so although the diversion of this underground water may not be equitable to all landowners.

When researching a property that borders a lake or sea it is important that you note this border. You must designate an exact description of the land and the areas of the land that border the lake or stream. You must also designate any item of record that you locate that either impairs or conveys the littoral rights to the landowner. If no specific record exists with regard to these rights, the underwriter will be aware of the statutes applicable to the property.

ACCRETION OR EROSION

Another factor that may affect the land, which borders an area of water, is accretion.

- Accretion is the process by which a piece of land is increased or extended by the gradual deposit of soil as a result of the action of a river, stream, lake, pond or mass of tidal waters that border the property.

- Erosion is decrease in the size of a piece of land through the gradual removal of soil.

Alterations to the original description may occur as a result of the accretion activity. This could alter the property description by adding additional land beyond that described within the records you are searching or with the removal of a portion of the land described though erosion.

When researching a property that a body of water it is important that you note this border. You must designate an exact description of the land and the areas of the land that border the body of water. You must also designate any item of record that you locate that modifies the original description of the property as a result of either accretion or erosion If no specific record exists with regard to accretion or erosion, the underwriter will be aware of the statutes applicable to the property. The exclusion or inclusion of insurance for accretions or erosions will be based upon the research your conduct.

Inclusion wording: *A portion or segment of the land being insured is a result of the process of accretion...*

or

The legal description of the land includes the phrase: together with all accretions appurtenant (abutting) thereto.

If the accretions of the property are to be insured you must

- Determine in a positive manner the existence of accretion

- Show that there is no avulsion – or sudden and perceptible change in the location of the body of water

- Obtain a recent land survey of the property that will allow the underwriter to draft an insurable legal description

- Compare the legal description of the property to be insured with the legal description of the property shown in the tax rolls.

  This allows you to ascertain if the property assessments are correct and that all taxes due have been paid.

If there is an issue concerning legal description and tax assessment, the title commitment will show the proper exception.

If the insurance will not cover the accretions of the property, the policy will show a proper exception or the language relating to the accretions will be deleted from the legal description.

When researching a title for accreted property you will need to obtain and file for record any boundary line agreements executed between the owner of the property and the owners of any property abutting the subject property. This agreement is in reference to the accreted land and all parties with interest must join in the execution of the agreements.

FLOOD PLAIN

When you are researching an area of land that borders any body of water, you must conduct research to determine the flood plain status of the property.

The designation of flood plain

- May have created limitations as to the uses that may be made of a particular parcel,

- May influence the perceived value of the property

- May make the property virtually unusable

A parcel of land need not border a body of water to be a flood risk. You should determine the potential designation of any property you are researching to ensure you incorporate any flood hazard risks associated with the property.

Flood designations are easily located within the public records you are searching or through the applicable agencies.

BEACH PROPERTIES

If a portion of a property you are researching contains beach area, other factors might affect the value of the property and the potential uses.

- You must research all applicable documents to determine whether if the government retains the title to the wet-sand area.

  The trust may designate the use of the beach property as public. In most cases, ownership of the publicly held area will not transfer ownership among private individuals regardless of the sale methods employed.

- You should also review all records to determine whether the public may have acquired the right to use any part of the beach area or any part of the upland for the purpose of access to the beach area.

  Adverse use or local custom may have granted this right to the public. If you obtain ownership interest to the property, limitations in your use rights may exist because of this custom or adverse use.

  Example: If the public has gained the right to use the beach area or the actual property for access to the beach area through custom or adverse use, the property might not be able to be fenced. This action would be limited because this fencing would limit the use of this access by the public.

When researching a property that borders contains beach area it is important that you note this border. You must designate an exact description of the land and the areas of the land that border the body of water. You must also designate any item of record that you locate that either impairs or conveys the rights to the beach property to the landowner. If no specific record exists with regard to these rights, the underwriter will be aware of the statutes applicable to the property.

CHAPTER

3

Estates

It is a large portion of your research function to determine exactly what parties may have obtained an interest to each right and interest of a particular piece of property. Multiple individuals may gain specific rights in relationship to the property. It is essential that you understand who has gained an interest and research all matters that those individuals may have enacted against the property.

As you have learned in the previous Chapters, real property transfers include a variety of rights and interests connected with each piece of real property. These rights and interests can be fully bundled and owned by one individual or may be segmented among a variety of interested parties. It is a large portion of your job function to determine exactly what parties may have obtained an interest to each right and interest of a particular piece of property.

The process of determining what individual might hold interest in the property and therefore have placed limitations on the property requires an understanding of the methodology of estate interests. Throughout history, basic systems have been used to govern the granting of land.

- **Feudal System**   Under the feudal system, a king owns all of the land and he is responsible for providing protection to the subjects who inhabit the land. This system is typically not one you will encounter in the United States. It is still used in certain portions of the world and the understanding of this system will enhance your overall understanding of the manifestations that have occurred to lead us to our present day system of land management.

- **Fee Tail**

A second system of estate interest known as the Fee Tail Estate was employed by the English Parliament to keep land ownership in the grantee family as long as a direct line of descent existed. A common name for this process is the process of entailment. This land governing methodology is rarely used within the United States. If you encounter the entailment processes within your research, it would be detailed as a restriction rather than applicable law.

In this type of estate, the grantee is often referred to as a fee tail tenant. This fee tail tenant is limited as to the actions he can take regarding the estate. The fee tail tenant is often limited concerning the rights to burden, convey, mortgage or otherwise encumber the estate. These limitations are in place to ensure that the estate remains within a family line.

Today you might see similar limitations with regard to the use of the land. A specifically recorded document will outline the applicable limitations. This document could affect the rights of the new titleholder. More information regarding such restrictions is included later in the coursework.

- **Allodial System**

The system used within the United States follows the pattern of an Allodial System. Under the Allodial System, an individual can own all land. They own the land in absolute independence.

The owner owes no rent, service, or allegiance to any government.

There are many types of ownership interest under our current system.

This system closely resembles the Allodial system but has a variety of categorical ownership types that you must understand. The variations detailed in the following pages are the most common you will encounter and it is important that you understand the ramifications of each specific type of estate ownership specific you will encounter.

Freehold Estate

A freehold estate is an ownership interest where one owns and possesses real property.

Ownership under a freehold estate is for an unspecified duration. A freehold estate continues until the owner knowingly relinquishes their rights and interest in the estate

- Knowingly relinquishing your rights and interests includes the failure to take actions such as paying real estate taxes as well as a specific act such as signing a mortgage and note.

- Your research should focus on all acts that any owner of the property may have taken that may inhibit the transfer of the full rights to the property whether these acts were active acts such as the enactment of a mortgage or passive acts such as the failure to pay taxes.

The concept of real estate ownership can be easiest understood when you view ownership as a bundle of rights or collection of rights to the ownership.

Fee Simple Estate

A fee simple estate is similar to the freehold estate and the two terms are interchangeable in some jurisdictions. The fee simple estate is the highest form of real estate ownership. Most of the property transfers in the United States use a fee simple estate transfer.

- A fee simple transfer simply means that the owner of the property enjoys the entire available bundle of rights.

- This type of estate is easy to transfer and is inheritable.

- This estate is the one that you will encounter frequently during your abstracting activity.

  When researching a fee simple estate transfer, you will verify actions taken on the part of the owner of record.

  If the owner has taken no actions that in inhibit or separate the full bundle of rights you may move on to the next item of research.

Life Estate

A life estate is a form of interest that is granted to an individual for a specific duration. At the end of the duration, the estate expires. The life estate grants a specific individual a life long right to use and occupy a specific piece of property.

- This grant to use the property is attached to the life or death of the designated party or life estate holder.

  The life estate remains in effect as long as the designated party is alive. Upon the death of the designated party, the interest granted through the life estate is nullified.

- Upon the death of the designated party, all interest in the estate will typically revert to the original grantor.

  The original grantor is termed the reversionary in the contract.

- At times, the terms of the life estate may dictate that the interest in the property goes to a third party upon the death of the life estate holder.

  This third party is typically referred to as a remainder man and his interest would be known as remainder interest.

When conducting research on a property that contains a life estate, you should research all actions applicable to the original grantor of the estate and the remainder man. The interest of the life estate holder will be a form of tenancy and as such, the life estate holder will not be legally able to encumber the property.

You should also determine the status of the life estate holder's interest. If the life estate holder maintains the current interest in the property, you should incorporate all of the terms of the life estate contract into your report.

Determinable Fee Estate

Similar to the life estate, a determinable fee estate grants the right to use the property to another based upon the occurrence of a specific event.

The estate grants the right to use and occupy the property to an individual until the occurrence of a designated event. In this case, the original grantor retains the possibility of reverter.

What this means is that if a designated event should occur, the determinable fee estate granting the property to the individual automatically ends and the property reverts to the original owner.

When conducting research on a property that contains a determinable fee estate, you should research all actions applicable to the original grantor of the estate. The interest of the determinable fee estate holder will be a form of tenancy and as such, the individual will not be legally able to encumber the property.

You should also determine the status of determinable fee estate holder's interest. If the interest remains at the time you complete your search, you should incorporate all of the terms of the estate into your report.

LIMITATIONS IN THE BUNDLE OF RIGHTS

In addition to understanding the types of estates you may encounter, you should also understand the division of rights that may occur in real property. The term describing the level of interest one has in the Real Property is a *bundle of rights*. The bundle of rights refers to the collective rights of ownership interest in a property that can be the owner of the property can hold. The owner of the various rights can be one or a variety of individuals.

It is important that you understand and research any limitations you may encounter that apply to the property you are researching. The abstract report includes the rights that are granted as well as rights that are limited in a real estate transfer.

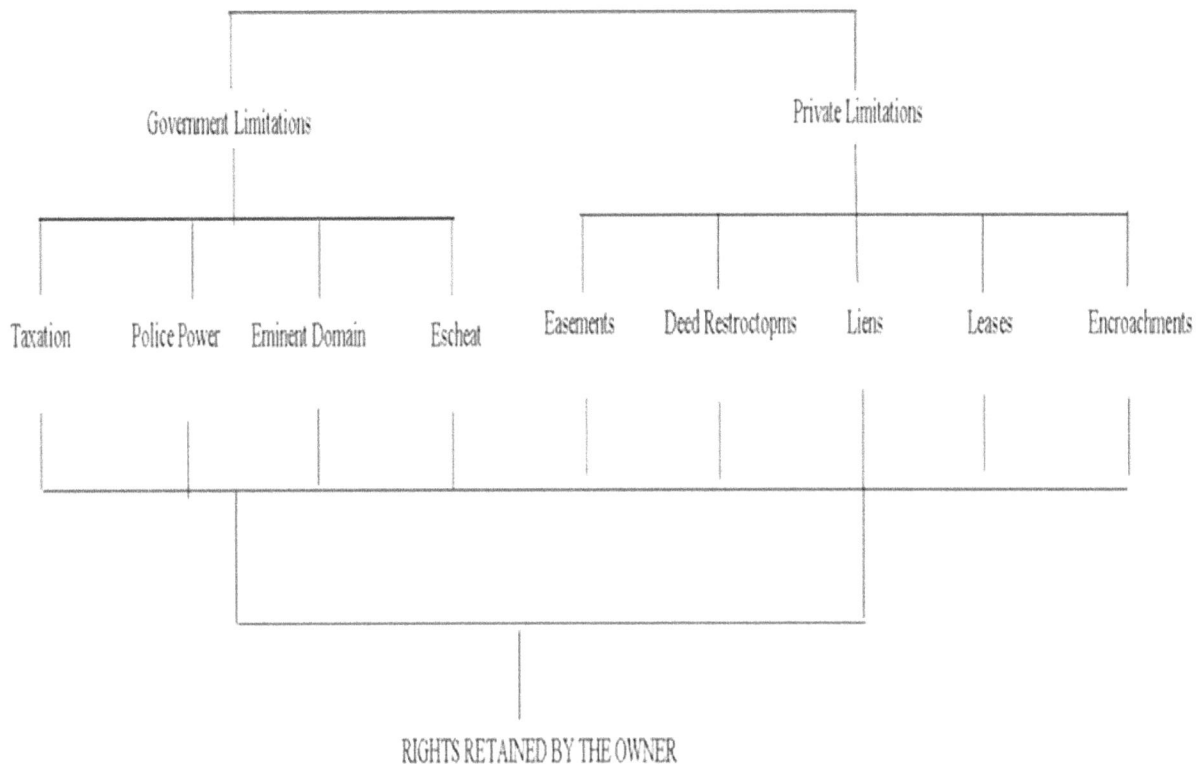

Figure 3:1 Diagram – Division and limitation of Rights

LIMITATIONS

It is easiest to understand the concept of real estate ownership when you view the ownership as a collection or "bundle" of rights that may be divided among one or multiple individuals. At the time of the initial grant, the bundle of rights is split into two parts. These are the government's interest and the individual owner's interest.

The government retains the rights to

- Taxation

- Eminent domain

- Police power

- Escheat

All the other rights associated with real estate belong to the property owner.

- The term for these rights is fee simple. The fee simple rights are available for private ownership.

- A person and his heirs can hold the fee simple bundle of rights for an unlimited amount of time.

Estate: The word estate is a synonym for bundle of rights.

Fee Simple: Fee simple estates can be granted to ones heirs and assigns in the form of an inheritance.

The fee simple estate refers to ones legal interest or rights in land.

Most real estate transactions are for the fee simple estate. In other words, when a person says he or she owns a piece of property they are typically discussing these fee simple estates.

The word title refers to this ownership. Any time someone besides the "owner" obtains a claim against a person's estate it becomes an encumbrance.

Encumbrance: An encumbrance is any claim, right, lien, estate, or liability that limits the fee simple title to a property.

Commonly you will find encumbrances that are easements, encroachments, deed restrictions, liens, lease, and air and surface right restrictions.

When researching the title in a fee simple estate it is important that you locate and note any encumbrance that may exist in the chain of title. These encumbrances may affect the title commitment and the ability of the new property owner to make full use of the land.

The removal of a "stick" from the bundle of rights or the imposition of a limitation of an owner's rights to the land can arise from either public or private sources. This removal limits the rights of ownership interest to the property.

GOVERNMENT LIMITATIONS

Government (public) limitations apply to all real estate and may come into effect at any time.

POLICE POWER   These limitations may occur because of police power. Police power enables the placement of limitations on the rights of a property owner in an effort to protect the health, safety, and general welfare of the public.

Examples: Zoning laws

Condemnation of a property

Verifying the zoning designation of a property is a standard research element of the abstract. You should note the specific zoning of the property within your abstracting repot.

- The zoning of a property can drastically influence its value.

- The zoning of nearby property may also affect the value of the subject property.

- Any owner gaining an interest in the property must comply with the specific zoning restrictions applicable to the property as well as any other use of police power that is evident concerning the property.

The government may create an easement against a piece of real property using government condemnation rights. An easement of this type can occur for a variety of reasons.

Example: A common government easement would occur when the government is acting to control a flood area and runs drainage pipe over or under the owner's property.

When an act of condemnation affects a portion of the land you are researching, it is important that you note all specifics of the action within the abstracting report.

The limitation will typically result in an exception in the title commitment and may nullify the title insurance company's ability to provide insurance coverage for that particular property. If you are unsure of the specific impact of a limitation that you note you should contact the underwriter assigned to your title commitment.

You should always provide a complete description of the condemnation act and in the case of the example, a map showing the exact location of the condemned area of the property. This exact description enables the title underwriter to incorporate specifics pertaining to the exception created by the condemnation within the title commitment

ESCHEAT   The government may also gain interest in a property through the process of Escheat. Escheat occurs when an owner dies and leaves no will or heirs enabling the property to revert to the state for disposal.

- You should note any transfers resulting from the process of escheat during the chain of title within the abstracting worksheet. This allows the underwriter on the commitment to note this issue in compliance with your specific company's regulations.

- You must determine the disposition of the property and continue searching the chain of title forward through time.

TAXATION   All privately held property is subject to the government right of taxation. Governments finance themselves by requiring property owners to share the cost of the benefits they receive from the government. The currently employed method of real estate interest assignment enables the government to retain the right to collect property taxes from landowners.

Real estate taxes are assessed against real property to support city, county, and some state services that are provided to the individuals living within the service area. Before the use of income tax, property taxes were the main source of revenue for the government and now are used in conjunction with the income tax revue to support all of the services provided to the community by the government.

Example: Schools, fire departments, police protection, public parks, and area libraries are all funded using public funding such as real estate taxes.

To ensure that property owners pay their real property taxes in the proscribed period, the right of taxation enables the government to seize ownership of real estate if taxes become delinquent. The government may then sell the property or generate a tax lien certificate to recover the unpaid taxes. The seizure of the delinquent property owner's interest by the taxing authority results in the loss of the owner's interest and a potential transfer to a new individual through a tax sale.

It is important that you determine the status of any tax liens that exist within the records of the property you are searching. Any unpaid lien may result in additional research requirements to determine the results of the lien.

- The government may abolish all of the interest of the delinquent property owner. This results in an offering of this interest at a tax deed sale. You would add the new owner to your search activity.

- The government may create a tax lien certificate that enables the investor to pay the face value of the taxes owed by the delinquent property owner. Following the purchase of the certificate, the investor will gain the ability to collect all of the interest and penalties that would have been due to the taxing authority if the certificate had not been sold. This investor would then become a lien holder of priority on the abstracting report.

These seizure options assist the taxing authority in ensuring the expected revenue for the operations of the different functions that they provide to the public. An integral portion of the abstract report you complete will be the verification of the status of all property taxes, municipal liens and other governmental matters.

EMINENT DOMAIN

Eminent Domain is the taking of a piece of private property for public use. The right of eminent domain is withheld from the bundle of rights by the government so that they may take ownership of privately held real estate for the benefit of the public regardless of the owner's wishes.

- The land may be taken for schools, roads, parks, urban renewal and other public and social purposes.

Other partially public entities or companies who provide specific services that are necessary to the welfare of the public may also use the power of eminent domain. This right is granted to enable the entity or company to enhance or further the service offerings provided to the public.

Example: Utility companies and railroads are permitted to obtain land using the processes of Eminent Domain.

- Eminent Domain may only occur with just compensation or payment for the taking of the privately held land.

- Eminent Domain occurs following a legal process called condemnation or a condemnation proceeding, in which the government condemns the portion of the land to which they require access or use.

- The property owner must be paid the fair market value for the property that is being taken from him.

- The actual condemnation is usually preceded by negotiations between he property owner and an agent for the public body wanting to acquire ownership.

> If the parties can arrive at a mutually acceptable price, the property is often purchased outright.

> If the parties cannot reach an agreement as to the value and price of the land, a formal proceeding is filed against the property owner in a court of law.

> The court hears expert opinions from appraisers and then issues a ruling as to the price of the property.

- This condemnation may be for the entire fee simple estate or for an easement that grants rights to a portion of the estate, typically in the form of right to access or come through the property.

> When only a portion of a parcel of land is being taken for use severance damages may be awarded to the property owner.

These damages are paid in addition to the payment for the land actually being taken.

It is important that you discover any actions of eminent domain that have occurred in relationship to the property you are researching.

You must take careful notes regarding any actions that were taken with respect to the property. These notes should include all pertinent information including

- Who obtained the rights to the land either a public entity or a partially public entity

- What portions of the land were affected by this action

  If only a portion of the land was affected, you must provide a full description of the area that was taken.

  - The dates of the actions

  - The names of the parties involved.

Only the property owner in possession at the time the condemnation occurs will receive compensation for the loss of the land that occurs because of the act of eminent domain

INVERSE CONDEMNATION   Another form of condemnation that may occur is inverse condemnation.

Inverse Condemnation is a form of condemnation that occurs when a property owner demands that his land be purchased from him.

Example: An inverse condemnation suit might occur if a property is located at the end of an airport runway.

The noise and pollutants created by the planes might impede the owner's right to quiet enjoyment of his property. This could lead to the property owner demanding that the airport authorities purchase the land.

In some cases, the land itself will not be purchased. If this occurs, the airport may be required to provide the owner with a damage award. These are called consequential damages and such damage awards will only be paid once.

Example: If a property is located near adjacent to a sewage treatment plant the owner might sue for consequential damages.
The property owner might suffer a loss of value due to the odors.
The property owner still has the use of his land but his enjoyment in the land and the value of the land is reduced.
The owner would therefore sue for consequential damages.

An inverse condemnation suit that results in the owner retaining the land while receiving a settlement figure for the loss of value would still enable the owner to transfer the deed to a new individual.

The issues that existed at the time of the inverse condemnation must be noted so that all matters are clear to the title underwriter and new property owner. It is important that you note all of the details of the suit as well as the outcome of the suit. The specific notation of the type of inverse condemnation, the outcome of the suit and the parties involved will enable the underwriter to correctly word the exception that will be incorporated into the title insurance policy.

EASEMENT   The government may take only a portion of a parcel of land in an effort to gain access to another area or place specific items upon that portion of the property. This separation of the land is known as an easement.

Easements may also occur privately.

Any owner gaining an interest in the property subject to an easement must remain compliant to the terms of the easement of record until certain actions occur that removes the easement.

The existence of the easement will affect the value of the property as well as the ability of future owners to make full use of the property. It is important that you review the section to follow regarding easements so that you may understand the limitations that may be placed upon the land that and the methods you must employ to locate the placement and removal of these limitations within the public records system.

When you encounter a document that enacts and easement against the property you are researching, you should note

•   The existence of the easement

- The exact location description of the easement

- The parties gaining and granting the easement

- The date of the easement

- Any special circumstance surrounding the easement

within your abstract report. This specific information will allow the underwriter preparing the commitment to word any exceptions that might result from the easement.

PRIVATE LIMITATIONS/ENCUMBRANCES

Private limitations on an estate are typically called encumbrances. The enactment of a private limitation or placing an encumbrance is commonly referred to as removing a stick from the bundle of rights. Examples of encumbrances are private easements, deed restrictions, encroachments, liens, and leases.

Easements

An easement grants the right to use, or partially use, all or a portion of the land of another individual. The easement does not grant ownership, just the authority to use the portion of the property described in the easement.

Easements may be granted by

- Grant by Deed

- Reservation in Deed

- Contractual Agreement

- Necessity

- Condemnation

- Prescription

Easements may be terminated by

- Release of the easement

- Expiration of the purpose of the easement

- End of prescription or the non-use of another's property.

- Merger of the dominant and servient estates

- End of necessity for the easement

When dealing with easements the estates affected obtain a secondary name.

SERVIENT ESTATE: A servient estate is the land on which the easement exists.

    SKILL BUILDER: The land on which the easement occurs "serves" the other property

DOMINANT ESTATE: The dominant estate is the land that benefits from the easement.

    SKILL BUILDER: The land that receives the easement is the land that dominates the use of the other property.

It is important to that you search all potential records in which the description of an easement may exist. Upon locating any easement, for or against the property you are searching, you should copy the document that grants the easement and include it as an addendum to your abstracting report. Any easement that exists, for or against the property you are researching, will affect the value, use, and potential of the property.

METHODS OF OBTAINING AN EASEMENT

**Deed Restriction/
Reservation in Deed** One method of obtaining an easement is with a deed restriction.

- The easement takes the form of a limitation placed in the deed by the seller.

- Deed restrictions place limits on the buyer and any future owner regarding the use, improvement, or maintenance of the land.

- Deed restrictions are often created to protect those who already have property in the area from a decrease in property values. This decrease could result from the construction of buildings, which are not compatible in value with those owned by the neighboring property owners.

Example: Scenic views may be impeded by the construction of a high-rise building.

This may result in a decrease of the value of nearby property.

A common deed restriction would be to limit new construction height to 15 feet.

The limitation restricts the buyer or new owner as to how they can use, improve, or maintain the property.

Deed Restriction limitations are enforced though the civil courts. The seller who placed the restriction begins the court action to enforce the restriction. The buyer or future owners are bound by this restriction until it is legally removed through a court action or through another viable method.

- A deed restriction is automatically deemed unenforceable if it requires the law to be broken in the enforcement of the restriction.

- Deed restrictions are usually difficult to remove because all affected parties must agree to remove such a restriction by signing a quitclaim deed.

It is important that you note the specific wording of any deed restrictions that affect the property you are researching. Certain deed restrictions may not be compatible with the new owners planned use of the land and others may affect the perceived value of the land. A deed restriction may be cause for a specific exception in the title commitment.

Necessity

An easement may also be created by necessity or condemnation.

An easement by necessity is the right or privilege of one party to use the land of another party for a special purpose. This purpose must be consistent with the current general use of the land and be necessary to the party receiving the easement. In case of an easement by necessity, the landowner is not dispossessed of his land; he simply coexists with the holder of the easement.

Common easements by necessity include those given to utility companies to run their lines over private property or the right of people to walk or drive across someone's land to reach another piece of property.

An easement by necessity occurs when the easement is necessary for the use of a person's property or land.

Example: If a seller sells the back portion of his property to a new owner, the back portion may be landlocked unless the buyer is given the right to access the portion.

This access would be obtained by traveling over the front portion whose ownership is retained by the seller.

The seller cannot land lock the new buyer so an easement by necessity is granted.

When conducting research, you must note any easement that affects the subject property. You should copy any document that refers to an easement, for or against the property and attach the copy as an addendum to your abstracting report.

Example: In the previous example, we showed an easement by necessity that granted the buyer of the back lot the right to gain access to the lot over the lot retained by the seller.

This right automatically becomes included in the sale if the back lot is sold or otherwise conveyed. The need to comply with the easement will also affect the front lot if it is transferred.

The effect on the front lot is often termed a burden. Whenever the front lot is sold or conveyed, the new owners must continue to respect the easement to the back lot. Any owner who purchases an interest in the front lot must to continue and respect the easement to the back lot. Similarly, an owner gaining interest in the back lot at would have use of the easement provided by the front lot in the same manner as the previous owner.

Example: An owner who purchases the front lot would not be able to erect a fence around the property. The erection of the fence would block the easement access granted to the back lot.

The front lot serves the back lot so it is termed a servient estate. The back lot would become the dominant estate.

The process of providing an easement granting access to the back lot is termed the granting of a right of way. The receipt or granting of any easement or right of way will become apparent to you during your research. Any documents referencing an easement of any type should be copied in their entirety and remitted as an addendum to the abstracting report.

Contractual

A contract may be created that provides a person a specific grant to an easement.

An owner may reserve specific rights or withhold rights of an easement in the wording of the deed granting the property to another party.

Example: A land developer might reserve easements for items such as utility lines or access to additional parcels when selling lots to a purchaser.

Any contract or special document that affects the property you are searching should be noted within the abstracting report. You should either include the exact wording of the granting clause or copy the contract to include as an addendum to your report.

Prescription

A method that may create an easement without a written document is called easement by prescription.

Prescription is the term for an easement process where the easement results from the open (observable), continuous (uninterrupted), notorious (public) and hostile (adverse to the owners title without the owners permission) use of the property.

In other words, this occurs when a person constantly uses a perceived easement over a specified period. If a person behaves in a manner that shows he owns an easement long enough, he will have made the ownership legal. This method of obtaining the legal right to the property of another individual is termed adverse possession.

Example: A neighbor uses a path built across the property you are bidding on to access the State Forest that abuts the property.

This use is considered to be open because they simply walked across the property.

The use is considered exclusive because it was the only method employed to access the State Forest.

The use is considered notorious because the neighbor made no effort to hide their access.

The use is considered hostile because the neighbor did not ask permission to use the pathway.

This taking infringes on the rights of the true and legal owner.

If the period prescribed by statute ripens into an actual title it is said to be possession commenced in wrong and maintained by right.

Simply stated, the initial possession of the property was notorious or hostile but the statute allowed the property to become rightfully owned by the new possessor.

Adverse possession is based on the applicability of the statute of limitations.

These statutes allow a specified time in which the legal owner may recover the property. If recovery is not completed within this time, the statute allows for the theory that the property has been abandoned to the adverse possessor.

For title purposes a title held by adverse possessions must be established by a final judgment or decree entered by a court of competent jurisdiction. This judgment or decree must not be available for appeal and must vest the title of the property to the plaintiff or adverse possessor. It is important that you confirm the status of this process as part of your abstracting duties. This will enable the underwriter to either accept the possession as fact or incorporate a specific exception into the wording of the commitment.

The laws of adverse possession vary by jurisdiction. When a non-appealable judgment or decree is obtained, a certified copy must be recorded in the record office designated by the statute.

Encroachment Another method of creating an easement is through the process of encroachment. Encroachment is the unauthorized intrusion of one's real property ON, OVER, or UNDER the land of another.

These encroachments may include:

- Tree roots

- Overhangs on Buildings

- Boundary line confusion when building

The property owner suffering the encroachment has the right to force the removal of the encroachment. If the encroachment is not removed within a certain time, it may then become and easement by prescription.

Any known encroachments should be noted in your abstracting report. It may be important to review documents of record pertaining to neighboring properties as part of your search if you find documentary evidence that leads you to believe an encroachment may exist.

Easement in Gross At times, an easement may be granted to a person or business that is not a neighboring property owner. This easement is known as an easement in gross, and in this type of easement, there is no dominant estate.

Example: A utility company is granted the right to run their lines over one's property.

These easements belong to the utility company and are no longer a part of the parcel of land.

All future owners of the land will be bound by the easement in gross.

An easement in gross may also be granted to an individual. These may include the right granted to a friend or neighbor to walk over the land of their neighbor to access a particular private spot.

In this instance, the easement in gross is for personal use and is not a transferable easement. The easement would end with the death of the person holding the easement.

The status of any easement in existence, the type of easement and the parties involved in the easement should be noted on your report.

METHODS OF TERMINATING AN EASEMENT

At times, you may encounter an easement that has been terminated. Understanding the methods of termination will assist you in deciding if a specific item you located is, in fact, an issue or if it has been resolved. Easements can be terminated by

- The release or end of the need for the easement

- The expiration of the purpose for the easement

- A merger of the dominant (the land which benefits from the easement) and servient (the land on which the easement exists) estates

- The end of the necessity for the easement

- In case of prescription, the easement may be terminated by the non-use of the property in a manner that is open, continuous, notorious, and hostile

It is important that you research the status of any easement that exists; against or in favor of, the property you are researching. This information will be included as part of your final abstracting report. You should either include the specific wording of the easement clause or copy the applicable document for inclusion as an addendum to the abstracting report.

CHAPTER

4

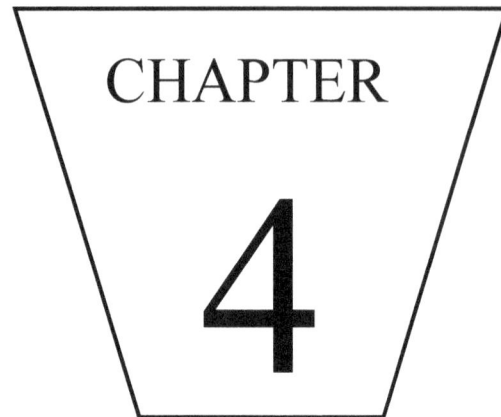

FORMS OF OWNERSHIP

When researching a property in the public records system it is important to understand the forms of ownership you may encounter. Earlier we emphasized that it is critical for you to search every owner who might have caused a claim to be made against the title of the subject property. In order to verify that you have adequately researched the actions of every owner, you must understand the different types of interest that exist.

R esearching potential encumbrances, liens and other defects established by the primary owner is an effective beginning in determining status of the title to the subject property. However, you must always remember the title might be affected by actions of other individuals with an interest in the property. Understanding the forms of ownership can assist you in ensuring that you have researched the actions of all owners.

There are varieties of ownership forms in existence and any owner may have created issues that must be carefully reviewed and noted on your abstracting report. Any action taken by any owner of record throughout the chain must be researched to ensure that there are no open issues left in the chain. If issues do exist that have not been resolved, you will need to generate specific notations on your abstracting report.

Sole Ownership
Sole ownership is also known as Tenancy by Severalty. This means the ownership is cut off from other owners or the individual owns the property alone.

In Sole Ownership, the term individual may refer to a variety of entities. Ownership must be a single entity but can include:

Married or single individuals

Corporations considered a single entity

Specific limitations and rights of ownership interests possible by unusual entities are detailed later in the coursework.

This form of ownership is both created and disposed of by deed or will.

When a sole owner holds the title to the property you are searching, you need only locate the matters pertinent to that owner to determine what matters might effect the value and use of the property. You should remember that actions of owners who held the property before the current one will also affect the uses and value of the property. You must search backward in time to determine the interest methodology used by each owner and then conduct the appropriate research.

Concurrent Ownership
Ownership may also be concurrent ownership. Concurrent ownership is the ownership of a property by two or more individuals.

These owners can share one of five different unites.

- Unity of Time
  They may have the Unity of Time, which means that both parties acquired their interest at the same instant in time.

- Unity of Title
  They may share the Unity of Title, which means that their interest was acquired by the same instrument.

- Unity of Possession
  They may share the Unity of Possession. This means that each party has the same,

undivided right to possess or use the property. In the Unity of Possession, all portions are owned equally.

- Unity of Interest

  They may share the Unity of Interest. The Unity of Interest means that each owner has an equal interest regardless of the amount they contribute or their desire to have different interests.

- Unity of Person

  They may share the Unity of Person, which means that each owner owns the property as a unity or team. An example of this would be a married couple forming one legal unit in the process of ownership.

Concurrent ownership may take many forms. These forms are referred to as a type of tenancy. Each tenancy will carry different rights that will affect the items you must research. The specific tenancies you may encounter during your research include

1. Tenancy by the Entirety

The parties united by the tenancy of the entirety are married individuals.

This is the only instance in concurrent ownership where the individuals will share all five forms of unity.

This form may be created by deed or will and may be disposed of only jointly by deed.

This form of tenancy does contain a right of survivorship. Right of survivorship is the right of the surviving co-owner to acquire the deceased con-owner's share in the property automatically.

If the parties in tenancy by the entirety are divorced, the tenancy by the entirety automatically terminates and then becomes a tenancy in common.

2. Joint Tenancy with the right of survivorship

Joint tenancy with the right of survivorship is held by two or more individual entities.

This tenancy shares all forms of unity EXCEPT the unity of person.

This form of tenancy may be created by deed or will and may only be disposed of by deed. Each individual may sell their share in the ownership without the consent of the other party.

This form of tenancy does contain the right of survivorship that means the remaining parties obtain the ownership interest of the deceased member upon his death. The right of survivorship defeats the effect of a will.

3. Tenancy in Common

Tenancy in common is held by two or more individuals.

The only form of unity required to create a tenancy in common is the unity of possession. There may be other unities in existence.

This form of tenancy may be created through deed, will, or divorce.

This form of ownership may be disposed of through either deed or will without the consent of the other party.

This form of ownership does not contain the right of survivorship so each individual may dispose of their interest at the time of their death as they choose.

When you are researching a title that contains a joint tenancy, all potential owners who might exist must be fully researched. Any owner of record who meets the requirements of ownership may have incurred liens, established precedent, conveyed, or created a condemnation with regard to the property you are researching. It is important to verify that the interests of each owner of record have been fully abolished and that the applicable records establishing this transfer of ownership are available in the public record.

AGREEMENT TO CHANGE TITLE FROM JOINT TENANCY
TO COMMUNITY PROPERTY

1. PARTIES:

Parties to this agreement are _____

and _____.

2. RECITALS:

a) The parties hereto are husband and wife, residing in the County of _____ State of
_____.

b) They have heretofore held property in their common or separate names, and may hereafter do
so.

c) They hold portions of their property in joint tenancy only as a matter of convenience or
transfer.

d) This agreement is entered into with the full knowledge on the part of each party of the extent
and probable value of all of the property and estate of the community, and of the separate and
joint property of each other, ownership of which would be conferred by law on each of them in
the event of the termination of their relationship by death or otherwise.

e) It is the express intent of the parties hereto that all their common properties are and shall be
their community property.

3. AGREEMENT THAT ALL PROPERTY SHALL BE COMMUNITY

Each party hereby releases all of his or her separate rights in and to any and all property, real or
personal and wherever situated, which either party now owns or has an interest in, and each
party agrees that all property or interest therein owned heretofore or presently or hereafter
acquired by either from common funds shall be deemed to be community property of the
parties hereto, whether held in their separate names, as joint tenants, as tenants in common, or
in any other legal form. The parties understand that this agreement will automatically, without
other formality, transfer to the other a one-half interest in any separate property now owned
and that such transfer could constitute a taxable gift under Federal and State law.

4. AGREEMENT MODIFIABLE IN WRITING ONLY:

This agreement shall not be modified except in writing signed by both parties, or by the mutual
written surrender or abandonment of their said community interest in accordance with the laws
of said State pertaining to the management of community property, or by the termination of
their marriage by death or otherwise.

Dated:_____ 20 _____

_____   _____

Figure 4:1 Sample Form – Agreement to Change Tenancy

SPECIAL OWNERSHIP CONSIDERATIONS

When addressing ownership and the rights of ownership, there are certain, specific entities and individuals whose ownership rights are further restricted or governed by law. Any person or legal entity who acquires interest in a piece of real property must be a bona fide purchaser. State law or judicial decisions determine the criteria for qualifying in as a bone fide purchaser.

BONE FIDE PURCHASER

Any person or legal entity that acquires an interest in property for valuable consideration and without notice of any outstanding unrecorded claims, defects, liens, or encumbrances may be considered a bona fide purchaser.

The conditions necessary to be considered a bona fide purchaser are established by state law or judicial dictate.

When the proposed insured does not qualify as a bona fide purchaser, it is necessary to show the exception in section B of the title commitment and policy. Title insurance companies will typically have available a complete listing of cases and situations in which an exception to the bona fide purchaser may be used.

You must establish that a bona fide purchaser holds the interests named within the public record. Any documentary evidence that exists should be noted on your abstracting report.

BUSINESS TRUSTS

A business trust is a form of unincorporated business organization where the trustees hold property. The property is managed and/or invested for the benefit of the holders of share certificates in the business.

Unless statute specifically allows the business trust to do so, the business trust may not acquire, hold, encumber, or convey title to real property in its own name. Any transfer or transaction must be executed in the name of the trustees.

You must ensure that the appropriate individuals executed any transfer or transaction within the chain of title that includes a business trust. Any research that exposes a business trust holding within the chain of title will require additional research to ensure that all transactions were executed properly.

CORPORATIONS

A Corporation is a legal entity created under state law. The powers, purposes, existence, limitations, and dissolution agreements are determined under the articles of incorporation for that particular entity.

> A corporation located within the state of incorporation is considered a domestic corporation.

> A Corporation in all other states is considered a foreign corporation.

By statute, a corporation is given the legal right to hold and deal in real property.

When researching a property held or to be transferred to a corporation, there are certain common items you should review. These are not all of the items that may require research, only the most common.

- Copies of the Articles or Certificate of Incorporation to determine the approved methodology for the ownership and transfer of real property

- Proof of good standing in the corporation

- Proof of good standing in the State

- Deed from former grantor conveying the interest in the property to the Corporation

- Judicial proceedings against the corporation

- Proof of stockholder's approval of the proposed transaction

- Limitations by State or Federal Law on the corporation's right to transfer or otherwise convey interest in real property

If you locate a transaction by a corporation within the title history of a property you are researching, you should extract the specific inclusions of the document and incorporate them into the abstractor summary. The title underwriter will review all of the applicable document inclusions and make a determination as to the legality of the transaction, specific exceptions that might exist and any additional research they will require to complete the title insurance issuance process.

BANKS AND SAVINGS INSTITUTIONS

Banks and savings institutions have a restricted capacity to acquire or hold real property.

The rights to hold real property are limited and are specifically designated by state and federal laws. These laws state that a bank or savings institution may acquire and hold bank offices and places of business. They may also execute and hold mortgages as collateral to a mortgagee's contracted debts, accept a deed in lieu of foreclosure or purchases at judicial sales.

Any other purpose for holding real estate property must be specifically authorized by law. Statutory law must be researched concerning state banks, state savings associations, and any other lending institution.

Any title insurance policy issued in favor of a bank or other savings institution must contain the exception concerning federal and statutory limitations imposed on banks, trust companies, and savings associations. These exceptions will be relative to the purchase, acquisition, and holding of real property.

If you locate a transaction by a bank or saving institution within the title history of a property you are researching, you should extract the specific inclusions of the document and incorporate them into the abstractor summary. The title underwriter will review all of the applicable document inclusions and make a determination as to the legality of the transaction, specific exceptions that might exist and any additional research they will require to complete the title insurance issuance process.

ALIENS

Property held by an alien is subject to statutory law of the state where the property is located.

- In some situations, a transaction executed by an alien will be subject to special reports and/or tax forms that must be processed.

- There may be restrictions concerning the rights of an alien to conduct real estate transactions through capital invested in legal entities or business organizations.

If you locate a transaction completed by an alien within the title history of a property you are researching, you should extract the specific inclusions of the document and incorporate them into the abstractor summary. The title underwriter will review all of the applicable document inclusions and make a determination as to the legality of the transaction, specific exceptions that might exist and any additional research they will require to complete the title insurance issuance process.

AGRICULTURAL AND FARM LANDS
REGARDING ALIEN OR ENTITY OWNERSHIP

Federal and state law subject agricultural and farmlands to various regulations, limitations, and restrictions with regard to ownership by either aliens or legal entities. The law of the jurisdiction where the land is located must be fully researched in order to determine what legal restrictions exist that may affect or limit the holding or ownership of the agricultural or farmlands.

Federally the applicable regulations are contained in part in the Agricultural Foreign Investment Act and Agricultural Credit Act of 1987.

The Agricultural Credit Act of 1987 also provides farmers with certain rights. In some cases, it provides the rights to farmers to reacquire or lease agricultural property that has been foreclosed or conveyed by deed in lieu of foreclosures.

If you locate a transaction pertaining to agricultural or farm lands within the title history of a property you are researching, you should extract the specific inclusions of the document and incorporate them into the abstractor summary. The title underwriter will review all of the applicable document inclusions and make a determination as to the legality of the transaction, specific exceptions that might exist and any additional research they will require to complete the title insurance issuance process.

GUARDIANSHIP

The term guardianship refers to the administration of the property and interest of a minor or incompetent individual.

Guardianship transactions are regulated by statute to ensure the safety of transactions conducted for these individuals. Procedures regarding transfer of property by a guardian vary by state. You should research the applicable statutes in your state to determine specific items of research.

If you locate a transaction enacted by a guardian on behalf of a minor or incompetent individual within the title history of a property you are researching, you should extract the specific inclusions of the document and incorporate them into the abstractor summary. The title underwriter will review all of the applicable document inclusions and make a determination as to the legality of the transaction, specific exceptions that might exist and any additional research they will require to complete the title insurance issuance process.

SPOUSAL OWNERSHIP

Unless specifically excepted by state law any spouse, even a non-owner spouse must join the owner-spouse in the execution of a real estate transaction.

Unless prohibited by a statute the spouse is allowed to execute a specific instrument that relinquishes all the marital rights to a property.

This relinquishment must be filed for record in the office designated by statute. You should note all specific details contained within this relinquishment document and consult with the underwriter assigned to the commitment. The underwriter will determine any additional research that may be required by the insurer.

ANTE NUPTIAL AGREEMENT

An Ante nuptial agreement is an agreement executed between a man and a woman before marriage, which settles future issues regarding

- The ownership of property

- Rights and obligations to property

- Dispositions of property in case of divorce

- Performance of marital duties

- The rights of other persons such as children and heirs to property

- Other conceivable agreements and obligations on the part of either party

When an ante nuptial agreement is discovered within the chain of title you are researching, all of details of the agreement should be included within your abstract report. You should research any additional related document that exists whether the document does or does not comply with the agreement.

A title company may occasionally rely on either an ante nuptial or prenuptial agreement for the elimination of the marital rights of a spouse. These issues should be presented to the insurance underwriter for review and determination.

POST-NUPTIAL AGREEMENT

A post-nuptial agreement is an agreement executed by the spouses after the marriage. This agreement contains the same content as an ante-nuptial agreement.

- To be valid both parties must be competent and enter these agreements in good faith.

- These agreements must be executed without duress, undue influence, or misrepresentation.

- These agreements must comply with all statutory requirements. They must also be filed for record with the real estate records office designated by statute.

When a postnuptial agreement is discovered within the chain of title that you are researching, all of the details of the agreement should be included within your abstract report. You should also research any document that exists whether the document does or does not comply with the agreement.

A title company may occasionally rely on either ante nuptial or prenuptial agreement for the elimination of the marital rights of a spouse. These issues should be presented to the insurance underwriter for review and determination.

CONVICTS

Convicts may be limited as to their rights to own, convey, encumber, will, or deed real property. When researching the property owned or formerly owned by a convict it is important to research the state law to determine the existence of any restriction or impairment imposed on the execution of real estate instruments by a convict.

If any restrictions are located, you must then determine the effect these restrictions will have on the transaction in question. Always forward a request for final determination to the title underwriter.

GOVERNMENT ENTITIES

When a real estate transaction is conducted by a governmental entity, it is important to scrutinize the processes to determine if the entity acted in accordance with statutory authority. You must determine some specific items.

- Whether the entity has the legal right to hold title to real property

- Whether law exists that empowers the entity to conduct a real estate transaction

- Whether all of the requirements, terms, provisions and conditions contained in the law governing the body have been met. There may be many items to research but the most common include

  That the transaction was properly advertised

That the property was sold to the highest bidder

That the authorized officer executed the agreement

That the type of instrument used in the conveyance is the applicable instrument

If the transaction required the consent or approval of another entity or group

If you encounter a transaction within the chain of title you are researching that was conducted by a government entity, you should obtain the details of all documents of record. Make certain you refer these items to the underwriter assigned to the commitment for a determination of additional items of research that may be necessary for the completion of the abstract.

INHERITANCE TRANSFER

When a person who owns real property dies or is otherwise permanently deemed unable to hold real property, certain laws and statutes effect the transfer of the property held.

All real property held by a person at the time of his or her death transfers immediately to the decedent's heirs by law. The laws of descent and distribution govern this distribution under the laws of the state where the property is located. When the assets of the descendent are located in different jurisdictions, the state of principal administration typically governs the distribution. Other states become know as ancillary administration states. You should familiarize yourself with the applicable statutes for your region or geographical area.

Of particular interest in the search process, are the individuals who gain interest following the death of a property owner and the payment of any applicable inheritance tax.

Inheritance tax is the tax imposed in some jurisdictions when a decedent receives property at the time of the death of the grantor.

Inheritance tax is different from the estate tax.

- The estate tax is the tax payable on the right to transmit the property upon death or in contemplation of death.

- The taxes imposed by transfer of inherited property are designated by statute. There are variances between states and jurisdictions and you should research the applicable statute for the region in which you will be conducting the search function.

If inheritance taxes due upon the transfer of ownership are paid according to the Statutes, no further action is required. If inheritance taxes were not paid at time title to the property was transferred, it is important that you locate and clearly note these unpaid items during your search so that the underwriter preparing the title commitment will be able to word the applicable exception.

If a person dies without a valid will or without having disposed of their property, the laws of Intestacy Property will come into effect. These statutes are known as the statutes of descent and distribution. They provide a system for the succession of property in the event the owner dies without a will or previous distribution. To research the chain of title subject to the laws of descent and distribution you should obtain a comprehensive understanding of the statutes governing the state in which you conduct the search. These specifics will vary by state and jurisdiction and the applicable coursework expansion material will be readily available from your jurisdictional resources. Specific advanced training in the individual state and jurisdictional processes is available.

Of specific interest to you during your research function will be the determination of any new ownership interest created either by will or by the laws of descent and distribution. This transfer of interest will provide you with additional owners who may have taken actions that affect the title to the property. Any new owner must be added to your search parameters and a determination of any outstanding actions taken by these owners must be incorporated into your summary.

It is important that you gain a comprehensive understanding of all of the different interests that may be created and terminated through the recordation within the public records system or through an action of Statute or Judicial decrees. This understanding will enable you to locate each successive owner within the records you are researching. Any action taken by any interested owner will affect the title to the property you are researching. The items included with each of the chapters you have completed should be viewed as applying to every owner with an interest in the property.

CHAPTER 5

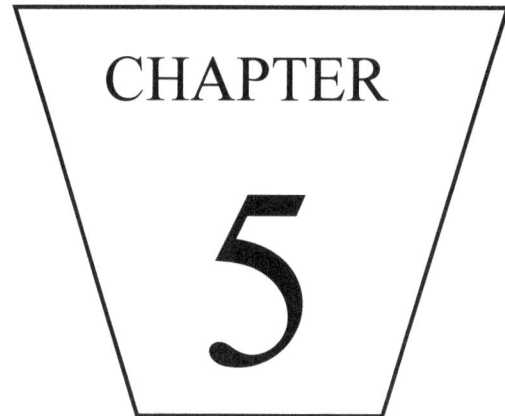

LIENS AND ENCUMBRANCES

An integral portion of your search will be research that centers on the various liens that may be in place against the property and their status. Liens will be among the most common items you will review during your career. Any lien that is recorded against the real property, the improvements, and fixtures or other items that pertain to the property being researched must be carefully reviewed.

W hen you are conducting research, you must research the status of any lien that you locate to determine if it can be collected or if it has been abolished through a proper procedure. This will enable you to determine the potential effect each lien will have on the transaction.

The first step in understanding how to locate and research potential liens against the property you are researching is to understand the types of liens that may exist.

Liens can be classified in two categories. These are the voluntary and involuntary lien. Within these categories may be two types of liens, specific liens and general liens.

VOLUNTARY LIEN   A voluntary lien is created when a property owner voluntarily creates a lien against the property in order to borrow money.

Example: A mortgage lien would be an example of a voluntary lien.

INVOLUNTARY LIEN   An involuntary lien is created through the operation or enforcement of the law.

Example: A property tax lien

A mechanic's lien

A judgment lien

An involuntary lien is often the result of inaction on the part of the debtor or a failure to pay as agreed.

Both types of liens will be recorded within the public records you are searching. Within these two categories are types of liens that must be understood.

GENERAL LIEN   A general lien goes against an individual and attaches to all of the real property of that individual in the county where the lien is recorded.

Example: Federal and state tax liens are considered general liens.

It is important that you search for any general liens that exist against any owner of record to the property you are searching.

To locate any general liens that exist in the chain of title, you will search the records by the names of all of the parties who have held ownership interest.

We have detailed the types of ownership interest that can be created to assist you in determining the names of possible owners.

You should conduct a search on each of these owners to assist you in locating any general liens that exist.

If a general lien exists against any owner of the property, you must conduct additional research to determine the status of these liens. If the liens still exist at the time of the search, you must make specific notations pertaining to the lien or remit a copy of the document granting the lien for attachment to your abstracting report.

JUDGMENT LIEN

A judgment lien is a lien on all of the debtor's property within the county or jurisdiction of the court issuing the judgment.

A judgment is defined as the final determination by a court of respective rights and claims of parties to an action or suit. The judgment becomes final depending on one of two factors:

1. The expiration of the time to appeal the judgment

2. Lack of a pending appeal

There are many types of judgments. The basic types are:

Declaratory
Judgment: A declaratory judgment declares the rights, duties, or status of the parties and/or expresses the opinion of the court on a question of law without ordering any action.

Money
Judgment: A money judgment orders the payment of money from one party to another

Federal
Judgment: A Federal Judgment is a judgment rendered in a federal court.

Foreign
Judgment: A foreign judgment is a judgment rendered by the court of a state or county different from the state or county where the judgment was brought.

Judgment
in Rem: A judgment in rem is a judgment on the status or condition of a particular matter and may not require any action.

Judgment
in Personam: A judgment in Personam is a judgment against a person not a judgment against a thing or right.

Dormant
Judgment: A dormant judgment is a judgment that has not been satisfied but has been in abeyance so long the execution cannot be issued without reviving the judgment. Another term is Expire Judgment.

- A judgment lien may only be brought by statue.

- A judgment lien may be brought against the property.

- A judgment lien results from lawsuits for which monetary damages are awarded.

Usually a judgment lien covers only the property in the county where the judgment is recorded but the creditor can extend the lien to property in other counties by filing a notice of lien in each of those counties.

The creditor awarded a judgment by the courts can request the courts issue a writ of execution. This writ allows the county sheriff to seize the property and sell a sufficient amount to pay the debt and the expenses of the sale.

If any judgment exists in the records with regard to the property you are researching, the status of the judgment should also be researched.

State law will dictate the required actions that enable a creditor to place a lien against the real and personal property of a debtor. Any judgments that exist within the public records pertaining to the property you are searching should be copied and attached to your abstracting report.

You must conduct research into the public records to

- Determine what judgments exist

- Ascertain the status of those judgments

- Note the potential obligations that are attached to the property being researched

TERMINATION

Judgment liens may terminate in a variety of methods. If you locate a judgment lien with regard to the property you are searching, you should research to determine if the judgment has been terminated.

The primary methods of termination are:

1. Lapse of time - expiration

2. Full payment and subsequent satisfaction of the judgment

3. Release of the real property from the lien by the creditor for whom the judgment was generated.

4. A merger occurs in which the creditor for whom the judgment was created becomes an interested owner in the property against which the judgment was executed.

5. Sale of the judgment

6. Vacation of the judgment

7. Reversal of the judgment in a court of appeal

8. The title of the property against which the judgment is placed is lost to adverse possession.

9. Provisions set forth by local statutes.

Other possible remedies resulting in termination are possible but these are the most common

If a judgment exists in the chain of title you are researching, you must determine the exact status of that judgment. You should conduct research to determine if any of the methods of termination of that judgment apply.

If there is proof that the judgment has been terminated you should provide the applicable information regarding the original judgment and applicable termination as part of your abstracting report.

If the judgment has not been terminated through one of the applicable methods, all details concerning that judgment must be included on your abstracting report.

SPECIFIC LIEN

A specific lien goes against a specifically identified property.

Example: A property tax lien is a specific lien because it is a lien against a specific piece of property and no other.

Mortgagees and mechanics liens are also specific liens.

These liens apply only to the noted property and therefore the failure to pay these liens cannot result in the forced sale of other property held by the debtor.

It is important to your search to determine what property a particular lien is held against and the effect these liens do or do not have on the property you are researching.

TAX LIEN

Tax liens are always paid first in order of priority. Tax liens may result from the right of the government to collect real estate property taxes.

- Each tax year, a tax lien is placed on the taxable property.

- This lien is removed when the property taxes are paid.

- If the taxes are not paid, the lien gives the government the right to force the sale of the property in an effort to recover their interest.

The processes involved in the sale of a property to obtain the funds required by the taxing authority vary by state and county.

- Some counties will sell only the lien they hold against the property.

- Other counties sell the actual deed to the property following a taxation foreclosure.

It is important that you familiarize yourself with the taxation recovery processes in your State so that you are aware of the possible liens and losses that may occur.

When a property is sold at tax sale, a special deed or a specific certificate is issued. You must research every action that occurred with regard to a tax lien issue against the property you are researching.

You must follow the chain of title through the tax lien or deed process to determine what individuals may have gained interest in the property. You will then continue the research processes by incorporating all matters pertaining to the new property owner into the abstracting report.

MECHANICS LIEN

The mechanic's lien law gives anyone that has furnished labor or materials for the improvement of a parcel of land the right to place a lien against the improvements and the land. At times, a mechanic's lien may usurp the priority of time. This lien may be placed when the owner of record does not pay services or materials used to improve the property.

To be entitled to a mechanic's lien, the work or materials must have been provided under a contract with the property owner or a legal representative of the owner.

Examples: Mechanics liens that may apply are water liens, utilities, and contractor services.

The theory behind the mechanic's lien is that the labor and materials supplied to the property enhance the value of that property. Consequently, the enhanced property should be used as security for payment. If the property owner does not pay as agreed, the lien can be enforced with a court supervised foreclosure sale.

If you locate a mechanic's lien against the property you are researching, it is important that you determine if any document exists, that satisfies this lien. If there is not a satisfaction on record with regard to this lien, you will need to provide the specifics of this lien to the underwriter assigned to the property. This allows the creation of specific instructions that may allow the title to be insured.

TERMINATION:

When you locate a lien recorded against the property you are research, you must conduct additional research to determine the status of the lien.

The lien may have been terminated through a valid action and such a termination act would appear within the records. Locating termination instruments within the records will enable you to remove the lien from your listing of potential issues that must be remedied or to incorporate the lien into the abstracting summary.

1. Payment or satisfaction

2. Release of the property

3. Assignment of the lien

4. Agreement between the parties

5. Statutory requirements

6. Expiration of the lien as determined by statutory regulation

7. Judicial discharge

8. Statutory bond

9. Dismissal of the suit

Other possible remedies resulting in termination are possible but these are the most common termination methods you will find when you are conducting your research.

MORTGAGE LIEN

The last form of lien that you will commonly encounter during a property search is the mortgage lien. A mortgage lien is created when the owner of property offers it to a lender as security against the repayment of a debt.

If the debt secured by the mortgage is not paid, the creditor can foreclose on the security property. Following foreclosure, the property is sold to repay the amount owed plus any allowable interest, penalties and other items.

If the foreclosure sale does not provide a sufficient amount of money to repay the debt, some states will allow the creditor holding the mortgage to petition the court to award a judgment of the balance still due.

You should search the public records for all mortgage notices. Upon locating a mortgage notice, you should conduct further research to determine if the mortgage was satisfied or if funds are still owed against the mortgage. Any funds that remain unpaid may attach to the real property that you are researching.

Any satisfaction of the mortgage will be on record for your review. You should note all mortgage details and applicable satisfactions that exist within the chain of title you are searching. This review should appear in reverse chronology on your abstracting report so that verification of the status of all mortgages held against the subject property at any time can be obtained.

LIEN PRIORITY

The priority of the liens is determined by time. The first in time to file or record a lien receives the higher level of priority.

Lien priority can also be determined by specific wording within the recorded documents notifying the public of the lien. This wording is often termed subordination clause and will dictate the status of the lien with regard to priority.

There are some exceptions to the priority by time and specific subordination clauses.

Example: A tax lien would be an example of a lien that would usurp the priority of time.

When noting any unsatisfied liens that exist with regard to the property you are researching, you should incorporate them into the abstracting summary in order of priority.

The priority will be established by reviewing the

- Recording dates on the lien

- Subordination or priority clauses incorporated into the lien

- Statutory regulations that dictate the liens that are able to usurp the priority of time

FORECLOSURE

A foreclosure proceeding is a legal procedure where the mortgagor obtains the real estate secured by a debt in default for obtaining the funds owed.

- The lien holder petitions the court for the right to sell the property to redeem the monies owed

- The courts and/or the lien holder notify any other individuals who hold interest or liens against the property of the foreclosure proceeding.

  This notice enables other lien holders to petition the courts for inclusion in the foreclosure process so that they may gain funds for any funds owed to them that are secured against the property.

- The court issues an order for the sale of the asset secured against the debt

- The real estate is sold to satisfy the debt

- The payment of liens at a foreclosure process occurs based upon the priority of the lien. The first in priority will be paid first from the funds received. Those liens holding later priority will only be paid if the funds received at the foreclosure proceeding exceed those required to satisfy higher priority debt.

- The specific provisions vary by state and you should familiarize yourself with the laws within the state where you will be conducting searches.

If notices indicating that a foreclosure exists in the chain of title you are researching, it is important that you conduct adequate research into the status of the foreclosure proceeding. You should also contact the underwriter for a determination of the applicable documents you must copy and the processes you must follow to finalize your search function.

The primary action that will be required of you with regard to a foreclosure proceeding is a determination of the satisfaction of all debt that was held against the property prior to the foreclosure proceeding and the obtainment of all satisfaction documents for each applicable lien. You should copy all of the applicable documents in their entirety and include them as an addendum to the abstracting summary.

EXECUTION SALE

In addition, to the other methods of obtaining payment for a debt owed, an execution sale may be conducted. An execution sale varies from a judicial sale in that no judgment must typically be obtained to execute a sale.

- A writ of execution is obtained giving the sheriff or other agent the right to conduct the sale to obtain a specific sum of money.

- Statutory law dictates whether this type of sale requires confirmation by the courts. You should research the law within your jurisdiction to determine the required actions for making this sale valid.

When an execution sale has been conducted in the chain of title being researched, you should consult the title underwriter for a determination of the type of sale and the applicable documents and processes you must research.

The primary action that will be required of you with regard to an execution sale is a determination of the satisfaction of all debt that was held against the property prior to the proceeding and the obtainment of all satisfaction documents for each applicable lien. You should copy all of the applicable documents in their entirety and include them as an addendum to the abstracting summary.

CHAPTER

6

DEEDS

When you are researching property at the courthouse, deeds will be the most common document you will encounter. The deeds that you will review will come in a variety of formats and types. Each deed will carry different warranties, covenants, and restrictions that will affect the title to the property and the potential uses of the property. Gaining a comprehensive knowledge of the format, inclusions and ramifications of each deed is essential to completing the research that will enable you to finalize the abstracting summary.

It is important to the success of your research that you understand the variety of deeds you will encounter. You must gain a knowledge base that enables you to review the deed to determine its purpose and effect, the forms of ownership that may be conveyed or relinquished by each deed and the warranties, covenants and restrictions that may be placed through the wording of the deed.

Deeds   convey or transfer the ownership interest in land from one person or entity to another. Conveyance may be either voluntary or involuntary.

A deed of conveyance is defined as a written instrument that is executed and delivered by an owner of real property for transferring title or interest in the property to another individual or entity.

The types of transfer deeds you encounter during your research will assist you in determining if further research into the past will be necessary.

Example: If you discover that the owner whose interest in the property you are researching

- held interest in the property solely

- gained the ownership interest through a fully insured, general warranty deed

- was required to comply with no restrictions as to the use or actions of the land

- retained the full bundle of rights to the property

You may only find it necessary to research the documents pertaining to the present owner's term of ownership. This limited search requirement will depend on the company for which you work. Some title insurer's require that a full search be conducted regardless of the apparent status while others will allow you to complete a bring down title, researching only the actions from the last fully insured search on the property.

Example: On the reverse, if you discover that the owner whose interest in the property you are research

- obtained their interest through a quit claim deed

- was subject to numerous land use restrictions

- segregated the mineral rights to the property with the intention of selling these rights to another party

You will wish to research the chain of title to determine the status of the many defects that are apparent. You will wish to determine:

- whether the owner in question actually held full interest in the property

- whether the ownership held was sole ownership or if it was shared with another individual

- that no obligations still exist from previous owners

- what land use restrictions still exist with regard to the use of the property

- that the sale is for the property rather than the mineral rights

The following explanations of the deeds you may encounter, the warranties, and covenants they may include and the implications of each will assist you in determining the depth of research you must conduct on each property.

GENERAL WARRANTY DEED

A general warranty deed is considered the highest form of deed that a buyer can receive from a seller and is the deed that you will encounter with the most frequency during your search.

The general warranty deed states that the Grantor (seller) warrants good, clear title to the grantee (buyer) and agrees to protect the grantee from any defect in the title whether the defect occurred during the seller's ownership or that of previous owners.

The essential component that makes this type of deed the most desirable to obtain is the warranty that title is a good, clear title throughout history and places the responsibility for defending any defects that may exist on the shoulders of the seller.

This is the most common deed you will encounter in your research and is among the most easily insured deeds from the perspective of the title insurance company.

GRANT DEED

A seller using the grant deed for conveyance provides warranty of a good, clear title only during his term of ownership and does not warrant the condition of the title prior to his possession of the property.

- In a general warranty deed, the grantor makes himself responsible for the encumbrances of prior owners as well as his own actions.

- The grant deed limits the grantor's responsibility to the period of time he actually owned the property.

The grant deed is similar in nature to the special warranty deed and will sometimes fall under the same terminology.

The location of a grant deed may imply that it is prudent to research all actions pertaining to the property that may have occurred both before and after the creation of this type of deed.

The mere existence of this type of deed does not guarantee that an issue exists, but it should be considered that the grantor creating this deed had knowledge of an issue that occurred prior to his ownership that he did not want to take responsibility for correcting.

The coverings of the grant deed are fewer in number and narrower in coverage than those found in the general warranty deed.

This applies especially to the covenant regarding encumbrances.

- In a general warranty deed, the grantor makes himself responsible for the encumbrances of prior owners as well as his own actions.

- The grant deed limits the grantor's responsibility to the period of time he actually owned the property.

The primary reason for the development and use of title insurance is the grant deed. Insurance coverage regarding the title gives the buyer protection if a flaw in the title is later discovered.

SPECIAL WARRANTY DEED

The special warranty deed is similar in nature to the grant deed. When conveying a property using the special warranty deed, the seller warrants the property title only against defect occurring during the seller's ownership and not against any defect existing before that time.

- Executors and trustees who speak on behalf of the estate often use the special warranty deed. The executor or trustee has no authority to warrant or defend the acts of previous owners of the title.

In some states, the special warranty is known as the bargain and sale deed.

In summary, the grantor warrants good, clear title to the grantee and agrees to protect and defend the grantee from all defects in the title that occurred during the grantor's ownership. In other words, the seller is guaranteeing that he has cleared the title from all defects during his ownership but is making no guarantees as to the condition of the title because of the actions of previous owners.

The ramifications of locating this type of deed in the records of the property you are researching are similar to those of the grant deed.

BARGAIN AND SALE DEED

The basic bargain sale deed contains no covenants and only the minimal essentials of the deed. The deed

- Identifies the buyer and the seller

- Recites consideration

- Describes the property

- Contains words of conveyance

- Contains the seller signature

The deed has no specific covenants incorporated into the wording. When conveying a property using the bargain and sale deed, the seller only implies that he owns the property described in the deed and makes no guarantees as to the condition of the title or even his or her ownership interest.

- The grantor implies that he owns an interest in the property but conveys the property without any warranty to the grantee.

In most cases, a buyer acquiring a bargain and sale deed will desire a full abstract or title search and the title insurance policy. If you are considering a career that includes a business of your own this type of deed is an excellent opportunity base upon which to establish your business.

QUITCLAIM DEED

A quitclaim deed has no covenants or warranties whatsoever.

The grantor using this type of deed is making no warranties nor are they even implying that they own the property.

Whatever right the seller possesses at the time the deed is delivered is conveyed to the buyer.

- If the seller has no interest or title to the property described in the deed no interest is conveyed to the buyer.

- If the seller possesses fee simple title, the fee simple title will be conveyed to the buyer.

The critical wording in a quitclaim deed is the seller's statement that he does remise, relief and quitclaim forever.

- Quitclaim actually means to renounce all possession or interest.

- Remise means to give up any existing claim.

If the grantor of a quitclaim deed subsequently acquires any other interest in the property, he is not required to convey it to the buyer.

Initially this type of deed may appear to have no effective use. However, situations often arise in transactions when a person will claim to have a partial ownership interest in a parcel of land.

Such an ownership interest is often discovered as a title defect or cloud of the title. These may result from an inheritance, community property, or mortgage foreclosure sale as well as from other means.

- The individual, who releases any claim to the fee simple title by enacting a quitclaim deed, would remove a cloud on the fee owner's title.

- The quitclaim deed can be used to create or provide relief from easements.

- The quitclaim deed can be used to release remainder and reversion interest.

- The quitclaim deed can be used to remove the interest of a party in a creative financing scenario.

The quitclaim deed is often used to clear an exiting blemish on a title and it is important to review the wording of the deed to determine the reasons the quitclaim deed was used. The exact clauses incorporated into the quitclaim deed as well as any applicable inclusions of the document that generated the need for the quitclaim action should be incorporated into your abstracting summary.

GIFT DEED

A gift deed is created when the phrase for money or other valuable consideration is replaced with the statement in consideration of his or her natural love and affection.

This phrase may be used in a general warranty, special warranty, or grant deed however; it is most often used in a quitclaim or bargain sale deed.

The location of a gift deed does not necessarily affect the method of search you may choose to conduct. However, the type of deed used in conjunction with the gift deed and the warranties and covenants included may assist you in determining additional or fewer research criteria that you should implement.

GUARDIAN'S DEED

A guardian's deed is used to convey a minor's interest in a property. This deed must contain the information that the legal authority usually, the court order, permits the guardians to convey a minors property.

**SHERRIFF DEED/
REFEREE DEED**

The Sheriff or Referee deeds are issued to a buyer when a person's real estate is sold because of a mortgage or other court ordered foreclosure sale.

This type of deed conveys only the foreclosed party's title and carries only one covenant.

- This covenant states that the sheriff or referee has not damaged the property title.

It is important that you review the title carefully when this type of deed exists. This type of deed frequently leaves unresolved issues in existence because a property owner whose property is taken by this type of action frequently has other matters against them that may affect the title to any real property they own.

**DEED IN LIEU OF
FORECLOSURE**

A deed in lieu of foreclosure may be created in an effort to avoid the full foreclosure action. The debtor conveys to the lender the property, including any equity, in consideration of the removal of all obligations to pay an agreed upon debt.

A deed in lieu of foreclosure may only be executed after the default on the part of the debtor.

It is important that you review the title carefully when this type of deed exists in the chain of title. Transfer using this type of deed frequently allows unresolved issues to remain in existence that may affect the title to the property you are searching.

CORRECTION DEED

A correction deed or deed of confirmation is used to correct an error in a previously executed and delivered deed. These can be used if an error was found in the spelling of the names or property description.

A quitclaim deed is often used to the same purpose.

A correction deed may also be called a deed of confirmation or a reformation deed. The accepted uses for this type of deed are extremely limited. This type of deed may only be used if item to be corrected is

- Clerical or Typographical

- A result of a lack of clarifying information

- To cure a defective acknowledgement

The location of a correction deed should be noted in that any alteration to any item included in your research listing might be cause for you to begin the search process again using the corrected information.

CESSION DEED

A cession deed is a form of quitclaim deed where a property owner conveys certain rights to the county or municipality.

When a cession deed is located, it is important that you note the owners whose interest is being transferred. Any other individuals who held interest at the time the cession deed was created will retain their interest after the cession deed.

The cession deed removes the interest of the individual providing conveyance through the deed into the future. Any actions that the owner took with regard to the property that pre-date the session deed must still be researched as they may still affect the title.

INTER SPOUSAL DEED   An inter spousal deed is used in some states to transfer real property between spouses.

The location of this type of deed may remove one owner of research from your listing because from the date of the deed creation forward, this owner will no longer be able to incur obligations against the property. It is important to remember that while you may cease researching for actions that occurred after the recording of this deed in relationship to the non-owner spouse, actions may still exist prior to the recording of the deed that might affect the property.

TAX DEED   A tax deed is used to convey title to real estate that has been sold by the government when the owner of record fails to pay the taxes assessed against the property.

The deeds you encounter vary greatly in nature, format, and inclusions. It is critical that you gain the knowledge you will need to review each deed applicable to your property and determine what rights or restrictions are incorporated into the document.

You must locate each deed that exists in the chain of title you are researching. All information contained on the deed must become a part of your abstract and some information may generate the need for the research of additional documents within the records system. The type of deed you are reviewing will often dictate the additional research you are required to perform. If you are unsure of the applicable actions required in relationship to one of the deeds detailed, you should consult with the underwriter that is assigned to the commitment.

- The wording of the deed will outline components that protect both parties in the transaction, restrict actions, or grant rights.

- A deed must contain some components to qualify as a recordable document under the guidelines of the recording requirements of the jurisdiction where the transfer occurs.

Parcel ID No.

File No.

This Indenture, made the _____ day of _____, 20 _____

Between

(hereinafter called Grantor) of the one part and

(hereinafter called Grantee) of the other part.

Witnesseth, that the said Grantor for and in consideration of _____ dollars ($_____) lawful money of the United States of America, unto him well and truly paid by the said Grantee, at or before the sealing and delivery hereof, the receipt whereof is hereby acknowledged, has granted, bargained, and sold, released, and confirmed, and by these presents does grant, bargain and sell, release and confirm unto the said Grantee, as the sole owner.

All that certain lot or piece of ground situate in _____ _____ being lot No ____, Page _____ being more fully described as follows

Bounded on the northwest by Pine street, on the Southwest by lot No. 200-17-21B (now or formerly of Mr. Jones et al); fronting twenty-five (25) feet on the Southeast side of First Avenue, between 3rd and 4th Streets and extending back at an equal width to a depth of One Hundred Twenty (120) feet.

Being known and numbered as Premises 322 First Avenue.

Being further identified as This County Tax Parcel Number 200-17-19A

Also ALL those certain lots or pieces of ground situate in This County in the City of Nod, County of There, and State of Freedom.

Figure 6:1 Sample Form – Deed Page 1

Together with all and singular the buildings and improvements, ways, streets, alleys, driveways, passages, waters, water-courses, rights, liberties, privileges, hereditaments, and appurtenances whatsoever unto the hereby granted premises belonging or in anywise appertaining, and the revisions and remainders, rents, issues, and profits thereof; and all the estate, right, title, interest, property, claim and demand whatsoever of him, the said grantor, as well at the laws in equity, of, in and to the same.

To have and to hold the said lot or piece of ground described above, with the buildings and improvements thereon erected, hereditaments and premises hereby granted, or mentioned and intended so to be, with the appurtenances, unto the said Grantee, here heirs and assigns, to and for the only property use and behoof of the said Grantee, her heirs and assigns, forever.

And the said Grantor, for herself and her heirs, executors and administrators, does, by these presents, covenant, grant and agree, to and with the said Grantee, her heirs and assigns, that he, the said Grantor, and his heirs, and against all and every other person and persons whosoever lawfully claiming or to claim the same or any part thereof, by, from or under him, her, it, or any of them shall and will.

Warrant and Forever Defend

In Witness Whereof, the party of the first part has hereunto set his hand and seal. Dated the day and year first above written.

Sealed and Delivered
IN THE PRESENCE OF US:

{Seal

Figure 6:2 Sample Form – Deed Page 2

This form is included for example purposes only. The form is modified from the acceptable real estate forms as released by HUD. The services of a real estate professional should be retained to ensure the correct forms are used for your transaction.

The following pages provide a sample of a deed parts with which you will wish to become familiar.

FORM The deed must take the form required by statutory law if any exists.

NAMES The names of the parties, both the buyers and the sellers, must be included on the deed.

Marital status and name changes should be included in this portion of the deed.

Name changes can be noted as *"formerly known as..."*

CAPACITY The parties to the deed must have legal capacity to enter a binding agreement as defined by statute.

CONSIDERATION A statement that the property is being sold for payment must be included.

This is the purchase price of the property.

In some states, you may maintain the privacy of the transfer by inserting a nominal amount of money plus other consideration a phrase such as *"$1.00 plus other good and valuable consideration"*.

Consideration may also take the form of a gift.

GRANTING CLAUSE The granting clause states what act the parties are performing with the endorsement of the document. In other words, this clause signifies the intent of the seller to convey his or her interest in the property to the buyer.

LEGAL DESCRIPTION The legal description is a very exact description of the property that will enable one to locate and identify the property to be conveyed and distinguishes the property from all other real estate.

RECITAL The recital identifies previous owners from whom the current grantor took title.

The recital will aid you in gaining information that will assist you in researching the chain of title.

REALTY TAX STAMPS Tax stamps are added to the document at the courthouse at the time of recordation. These stamps provide proof of the payment of the state and local taxes due when transferring real estate have been paid.

TO HAVE AND TO HOLD CLAUSE

Also known as the Habendum, the have and to hold clause is the technical language that describes the ownership interest in the property that is being transferred through the enactment of the deed.

GRANTOR'S SIGNATURE

The grantors (sellers) must sign the deed.

The grantee (buyer) does not need to sign the deed)

ACKNOWLEDGEMENT

Acknowledgement is best known as notarizing. This is the event where the sellers appear before a notary or other approved person to prove and declare that the signing of the deed and the transfer of the deed is a voluntary act.

CERTIFICATE OF GRANTEE'S ADDRESS

The certificate of address is a requirement that must be incorporated into the deed document in order to record the deed. It provides the information applicable to the new owners such as full name and address and enables the taxing authorities to send all future notices and tax bills to the grantee.

RECORDING REFERENCE

The recording reference is added by the clerk off record and it specifies the date, deeds book volume, and deed-book page number where the recorded document is filed.

DELIVERY AND ACCEPTANCE

While there is no requirement that the grantees sign the deed document, the last legal step in the transfer of the deed is the delivery and acceptance of the conveyance. The grantee must receive and accept the document. This acceptance finalizes the transaction and conveyance of the property has been achieved.

Delivery may be actual or constructive.

ACTUAL DELIVERY is the physical transfer of the deed before the death of the grantor.

CONSTRUCTIVE

DELIVERY   is the delivery in cases where the law implies the existence of delivery by the conduct of the parties involved.

The deed example incorporated before the form explanation shows the form and inclusions of a general warranty deed. The general warranty deed is considered the highest form of a deed that a buyer may obtain. These will be among the most common deeds you will encounter within the courthouse records. You will also encounter many deeds that contain limited warranties, covenants, and specifics. The legal form of these deeds will be patterned in the same manner as the General Warranty Deed; however, the inclusions will differ dramatically. The following page includes a sample of a tax deed. You should compare the two deeds to gain a better understanding of the inclusions of each type of deed that you may encounter during your research activity.

Parcel ID No.

File No.

JUDIICAL SALE IN CONNECTION WITH THE TAX SALE OF 20____

DEED

OF

TAX CLAIM BUREAU OF ANY COUNTY, ANYWHERE

Made the _____ day of _____, Two Thousand _____ (20___)

Between the TAX CLAIM BUREAU OF _____ COUNTY (the latter a subdivision of the City of _____ with a seat of government in the Borough of _____ County of _____ and Commonwealth of _____) as constituted and created by virtue of the provisions of the Act of Assembly approved the 7th day of July, 1947, P.L. 1368 (72 PS 5860.101) and known as the "Real Estate Tax Sale Law" as supplemented and amended, as trustee for

Owner or reputed owners, herein designated as Grantor of Party of the First Part;

AND

of the City of _____, County of _____, and Commonwealth or State of _____, herein designated as Grantee or Party of the Second Part;

Figure 6:3 Sample Form – Tax Deed Page 1

Witnesseth THAT WHEREAS, the real estate hereinafter identified was exposed to the Tax Sale duly held by the First Party on the ____ day of _____, 20 ___, as continued, adjourned, or readjourned, under and by virtue of the provisions of the Act of Assembly hereinbefore identified and the upset price was not bid by anyone is such Sale; and

WITNESSETH, THAT WHEREAS, by proceedings filed to No. _____ a Decree of the Court of Common Please of _____ County, was entered directing that said property be sold at a subsequent date fixed by the Court, free and clear of all tax and municipal claims, mortgages, liens, charges, and estates, of whatsoever kind, with the purchaser at said sale to have an absolute title to said property, free and clear of the claims aforesaid;

AND WHEREAS, the Second Party became the purchaser, (or is the heir or assignee of said purchaser) of said real estate at the Judicial Sale held by the First Party on the _____ day of _____ A.D. 20 ___, as continued, adjourned, or readjourned, under and by virtue of the provisions of the Act of Assembly hereinbefore identified.

NOW, THEREFORE, WITNESSETH, that under and in pursuance of the Act of Assembly aforesaid and the Order of Court entered in connection, therewith, and for and in consideration of $_____ _____ Dollars, in hand paid, the receipt of which is herewith acknowledged, (being the price bid at said Judicial Sale), the receipt of which is herewith acknowledged, (being the price bid at said Judicial Sale), the Grantor or Party of the First Part, under and by virtue of the Act of Assembly aforesaid as Trustee for the owner or reputed owner of said Real Estate, does hereby grant, bargain, sell, assign, and release, in fee simple, unto the said Grantee or Party of the Second Part, their heirs, successors, and assigns,

> ALL

> Control # 060-0027

> Map # 0800-21-17B

For chain of title see DBV 1128 page 116

> All taxes up to and including 20____ County and Township were in sale.

> Realty transfer tax is $_____ for 1% Local and $_____ for 1% State, based on the
Common Level Ratio Factor at the time of the sale, which was 11.91%.

TO the end that said purchaser shall take and hold an absolute title to the said property free and clear of all tax and municipal claims, mortgages, liens, charges, and estates of whatsoever kind, except ground rent separately taxed.

TO HAVE AND TO HOLD the said premises, without warranty of any kind or nature, unto the said Party of the Second Part, their heirs, successors, and assigns forever.

IN WITNESS WHEREOF, the said Party of the First Part set its hand and seal the day and year aforesaid.

TAX CLAIM BUREAU OF

Figure 6:4 Sample Form – Tax Deed Page 2

WARRANTIES OF TITLE

A deed that meets of all the legal requirements of recordation could leave some questions unanswered.

- The grantor will include certain covenants and warranties in the deed.

- Specific covenants and warranties that are written promises by the grantors regarding the condition of the title may be included in the deed.

- The grantor may also guarantees that if the title is not as stated he or she will compensate the grantee for a loss suffered.

Five different covenants have evolved over the centuries for use in deeds. The inclusion of any of these covenants could provide additional assurance to you with regard to the condition of the title at the time the deed was created.

The deeds you review may contain none, some, or all of these covenants and warranties. Additional warranties may exist within the jurisdiction in which you conduct your search. It is an essential portion of the job of the abstractor to obtain a full understanding of these guarantees. These guarantees, like the specific deed types named earlier in this chapter, will assist you in determining what additional items of research you may need.

COVENANT OF SEIZIN	under the covenant, a Seizin the grantor guarantees that he is the owner and possessor of the property being conveyed and that the seller actually has the right to convey the property.
COVENANT OF ENJOYMENT	Under the covenant of enjoyment, the sellers warranty or guarantee that the buyer will not be disturbed by someone else who might claim an interest in the property.
COVENANT AGAINST ENCUMBRANCES	The covenants against encumbrances is when the seller guarantees to the buyer that the title is not encumbered with any easements, restrictions, unpaid property taxes, assessments, mortgages, judgments, etc. except as stated in the deed. If the buyer discovers an undisclosed encumbrance, he can sue the seller for the cost of removing it.
COVENANT OF FURTHER ASSURANCE	The covenant of further assurance requires the seller to procure and deliver to the buyer any subsequent documents that might be necessary to make good the buyer's title.

WARRANTY DEED FOREVER Warranty deed forever is the guarantee to the buyer that the seller will bear the expense of defending the buyer's title. If at any time in future, someone else attempts to and is able to prove that he is the rightful owner of the property, the seller will bear the burden of the costs incurred. The buyer can sue the seller for damages up to the value the property.

Because the warranties that might be included within a deed could prove costly if an issue becomes apparent in the future, the seller often backs them up with title insurance.

COVENANT OF RIGHT TO CONVEY The covenant of the right to convey is an assurance that the grantor has the right to convey the property to the grantee. In some jurisdictions, this warranty is covered under the covenant of seizin.

COVENANT OF NON-CLAIM The convent of non-claim assures the grantee that neither the grantor nor his heirs or assigns will claim any title to the property being conveyed.

Before title insurance is issued, it is the abstractor's job to confirm the needed covenant or warranty is included within the deed of record. It is standard practice to have the seller appear before a notary public or other public officer and formally declare that he filed the deed voluntarily. This appearance is his acknowledgment.

The more covenants and warranties the seller includes in the deed of conveyance the more solid the transfer can be considered. The specific insurer who is underwriting the title insurance for the title you are researching will establish the minimum requirements they must have with regard to warranty and covenant inclusions. You must ensure that the applicable warranty or covenant exists within the deed or additional action or exceptions may be required on the title commitment.

LIMITATIONS IN THE DEED

At times, the deed may contain limitations regarding the rights and interests being transferred to the buyer or the actions the buyer may take in the future regarding the piece of property. These limitations can vary depending on the specific situation and the needs of the parties. These limitations typically affect not only the buyer named in the deed that contains the limitation, but all future owners. You must provide a detailed description of any limitations that you note during your search. In general, limitations take one of three forms.

EXCEPTION Exceptions withhold or exclude a part of the estate being conveyed from transfer through the transaction and represent specific property rights that are not being granted to the buyer.

Example: A common exception would be if the grantor required the use of an easement across a portion of his property being sold or conveyed to access another portion of his property that is being retained.

An exception of this type will be shown as an exception Schedule B of the title commitment. When you locate an exception within the chain of title, you must provide the exact wording of the exception as well as the specifics of the document that contains the exception. This helps to ensure the proper wording of the exception created on the title commitment. You should also scrutinize any future documents created to determine if alterations exist that might modify or abolish this exception.

RESERVATION

Reservations are clauses that reserve an interest in the title being conveyed. Reservations are created in the favor of the grantor.

Example: A common reservation would when the seller wishes to retain the mineral rights of the property.

These reservations will be shown as an exception Schedule B of the title commitment. When you locate a reservation within the chain of title, you must provide the exact wording of the reservation as well as the specifics of the document that contains the reservation. This helps to ensure the proper wording of the exception created on the title commitment. You should also scrutinize any future documents created to determine if alterations exist that might modify, transfer, or abolish this reservation.

RESTRICTIONS

Restrictions may be incorporated into the deed as a limitation on the future action a buyer may take with the property.

Example: A common restriction would be to limit new construction on the property to buildings of less than 15 feet in height. This restriction would protect the scenic views of other property owners in the area.

These restrictions will be shown as an exception Schedule B of the title commitment. When you locate a restriction within the chain of title, you must provide the exact wording of the restriction as well as the specifics of the document that contains the restriction. This helps to ensure the proper wording of the exception created on the title commitment. You should also scrutinize any future documents created to determine if alterations exist that might modify or abolish this restriction.

Each entry on the deed and the specific wording, inclusions and type of deed within the public records of the property you are researching will affect the rights of any future owner of that property. It is essential that you review each deed document. You will note any specific items within the wording of the deed that must be noted on the abstracting summary.

The actual form of the deeds you will review will vary. Each State and Jurisdiction will have variations within the form of the deeds you will see. Deed form has altered through the years causing still more variety. Providing all of the legal components exist, any individual may create their own deed without seeking the aid or advice of a legal professional.

We have included an example of a quitclaim deed on the following pages. You should compare the quitclaim deed inclusions and exclusions with the other deed samples. This comparison will enable you to isolate the form of each potential deed you will encounter and learn to determine what covenants, warranties and transfer restrictions are being placed with the recording of the applicable document.

Hennin

Recorder's Use Only

QUITCLAIM DEED

FOR A VALUABLE CONDIERATION.   HEREBY QUITCLAIM to:

The real property in the County of _____, State of _____ described as

Witness my hand this _____ day of _____, 20 ____.

_____   _____

State of   }   Witness my hand and official seal:

County of   }
On _____, 20___   _____
Before me, the undersigned, a Notary Public   Notary Public in and for Said County and State
and for said County and State personally
appeared   NOTARY SEAL

Proved to me on the basis of satisfactory evidence to be the
person whose name is (are) sub-scribed to the instrument and
acknowledge that

executed the same.

Figure 6:5 Sample Form – Quit Claim Deed

This form is included for example purposes only. The form is modified from the acceptable real estate forms as released by HUD. The services of a real estate professional should be retained to ensure the correct forms are used for your transaction.

CHAPTER

7

UNDERSTANDING CONTRACTS

In addition to the deeds, you will review other legal documents during your search. Each document may limit the rights and interests in the property. It is essential that you gain a comprehensive understanding of the actions that are being taken with the recordation of the contract, the termination processes for each contract and the implications that each contract carries with regard to the bundle of rights and research you will be required to complete.

A real estate sales contract is the document or instrument that outlines all of the terms and conditions of the sale between a seller and a buyer. These agreements may be referenced under several names such as:

- Offer to Purchase

- Option to Buy or Sell

- Sales Agreement

- Contract of Purchase of Real Estate

- Contract for Deed

- Other variations as accepted

The terminology of naming these contracts is subject to jurisdictional variances.

Not all real estate sales contracts are recorded at the courthouse of record, but if the existence of such a contract is known, the contract and potential resulting actions against the property must be considered during the period of search.

The period between the execution of the sales agreement and the delivery of the deed creates an interest known as equitable title. During this time, the buyer has an interest in the property.

Any contract of sale must be noted and shown as an exception on Schedule B of the title commitment and policy.

If the contractual rights have been terminated the exception may not be necessary.
To terminate the rights of a contract of sale there must be:

- Proof of acquisition of the property by the buyer

- A recorded instrument dated later in time than the agreement terminating the contract and releasing the property from the terms and conditions of the contract.

- A judicial decree terminating the contract. This decree must not be subject to appeal.

Real Estate Title Search - Abstracting

STANDARD AGREEMENT FOR THE SALE OF REAL ESTATE

SELLERS BUISNES RELATIONSHIP WITH LICENSED BROKER
Broker (company) _____ Phone _____
Address _____ Fax _____
Licensee(s) _____ Designated Agent __ Yes __ No
BROKER IS THE AGNET FOR THE SELLER   OR (if checked below):
Broker is NOT the Agent for the seller and is a/an: __ AGENT FOR BUYER __ Transaction Licensee

BUYERS BUISNES RELATIONSHIP WITH LICENSED BROKER
Broker (company) _____ Phone _____
Address _____ Fax _____
Licensee(s) _____ Designated Agent __ Yes __ No
BROKER IS THE AGNET FOR THE BUYER   OR (if checked below):
Broker is NOT the Agent for the seller and is a/an: __ AGENT FOR SELLER __ Transaction Licensee

When the same Broker is Agent for Buyer, Broker is a Dual Agent. All of Broker's licensees are also Dual Agents UNLESS there is a separate Designated Agents for Buyer and Seller. If the same Licensee is designated for Seller and Buyer, the Licensee is a Dual Agent.

1. ***This Agreement***, dated _____ is between SELLER(S):
_____, called Seller, and
BUYER(S): _____ , called Buyer.

2. PROPERTY Seller herby agrees to sell and convey to Buyer, who hereby agrees to purchase:
ALL THAT CERTAIN lot or piece of ground with buildings and improvements thereon erected, if any, known as:
_____
_____
In the _____ of _____ County of _____ in the State of
_____. Identification (e.g., Tax ID#, Parcel #; Lot, Block; Deed Book, Page, Recording Date): _____

3. TERMS
(A) Purchase Price _____
_____ U.S. Dollars
which will be paid to the Seller by the Buyer as follows:
1. Cash or check at the signing of this Agreement_____ $ _____
2. Cash or check within ____ days of the execution of this agreement_____ $ _____
3. _____ $ _____
4. Cash or cashiers check at the time of settlement_____ $ _____
TOTAL $ _____

(B) Deposits paid by Buyer within ____ DAYS of settlement will be by cash or cashiers check. Deposits, regardless of the form of payment and the person designated as payee, will be paid in U.S. Dollars to Broker for Seller (unless otherwise stated here) _____ who will retain deposits in an escrow account until consummation or termination of this Agreement in conformity with all applicable laws and regulations. Any check tendered as deposit monies may be held uncashed pending the acceptance of this agreement.

(C) Seller's written approval to be on or before _____

(D) Settlement to be on _____ or before if Buyer and Seller agree

(E) Settlement will occur in the county where the Property is located or in an adjacent county, during normal business hours, unless Buyer and Seller agree otherwise.

(F) Conveyance from Seller will be by fee simple deed of Special Warranty unless otherwise stated here _____

(G) Payment of transfer taxes will be divided equally between Buyer and Seller unless otherwise stated here _____

(H) At the time of settlement, the following will be adjusted pro-rata on a daily basis between Buyer and Seller, reimbursing where applicable current taxes (see Information regarding Real Estate Taxes), rents, interest on mortgage assumptions, condominium fees, and homeowner's association fees, water and or sewer fees together with any other lienable municipal services.

Figure 7:1 Sample Form – Real Estate Purchase Agreement Page 1
This form is included for example purposes only. The form is modified from the acceptable real estate forms as released by HUD. The services of a real estate professional should be retained to ensure the correct forms are used for your transaction.

CONTRACT FOR DEED

A contract for deed is a method of purchasing a property using a specific finance methodology. Contract for deed is also sometimes termed:

- Land Contract

- Installment Land Contract

- Article of Agreement

- Other terms as have become common in a specific region or jurisdiction

Under a contract for deed:

- The seller retains the legal title to the property.

- The buyer takes possession of the property and obtains equitable title.

- The buyer makes regular monthly payments to the seller over an agreed upon term.

- The seller is not required to deliver the deed to the buyer until all terms of the sales contract have been met.

- During the contract term, both parties may assign their interest in the property and the transaction.

These types of transactions are subject to statute and jurisdictional variations. If such a contract exists, it is important to note the:

- Contracts existence

- Contract parties

- Condition of the contract

If such a contract exists in record and no termination of the contract is evident, the contract must be shown as an exception on Schedule B on the title commitment and policy. When you locate a contract of this type within the chain of title, you must provide the exact wording of the contract as well as the specifics of the contract. This helps to ensure the proper wording of the exception created on the title commitment. You should also scrutinize any future documents created to determine if alterations exist that might modify, satisfy, transfer, or abolish this contract.

If a contract such as this exists in the chain of title, there are certain methods by which the contract may have been terminated. You should review all possible records to determine if such a termination exists. If the contract has not been terminated but an exception to the title is not desirable, then certain actions must be taken to nullify the contract. These may include:

TERMINATION An executed document from the buyer must be obtained that releases and/or conveys the rights of the vendee or buyer in the contract.

A vendor/sellers declaration of forfeiture of the contract is not typically sufficient for the nullification of such a contract and the subsequent exceptions created.

A judicial decree that is not subject to appeals may be obtained. This decree must declare the forfeiture and nullification of the contract.

Under this type of contract, the interest of either party in the property may allow a mortgage to be obtained. You should conduct your search under the assumption that a mortgage exists under either party.

Land Contract

This Agreement is made and entered into by and between _____ (seller), whose address is,_____
hereinafter called the Vendor and _____ (buyer) whose address is _____
hereinafter called the Vendee.

Witnesseth: The Vendor, for himself, his heirs and assigns, does hereby agree to sell to the Vendee, their heirs and assigns, the following real estate commonly known as:_____
_____ and further described; as _____
_____together with all appurtenances, rights, privileges, easements, and all buildings and fixtures in their present condition located upon said property.

1. CONTRACT PRICE METHOD OF PAYMENT, INTEREST RATE:
    In consideration whereof, the Vendee agrees to purchase the above-described property for the sum of
    _____ Dollars
    ($_____), payable as follows:

    The sum of $_____ as initial consideration at the time of
    execution of the within Land Contract, the receipt of which is hereby acknowledged, leaving a
    principal balance owed by Vendee of $_____ together with interest on the unpaid
    balance payable in consecutive monthly installments of $_____ beginning on the
    _____ day of _____ 20___, and on the _____ day of each and every month thereafter
    until said balance and interest is paid in full, or until the _____ day of _____
    20_____
    at which time the entire remaining balance plus accrued interest shall become due and payable.

Figure 7:2 Sample Form – Land Contract Agreement Page 1

The interest on the unpaid balance due hereon shall be (_____ %) percent annum computed monthly, in accordance with a month amortization schedule during the life of this agreement.

Payments shall be credited first to the interest. The remainder to the principal or other sums due Vendor. The total amount of this obligation, both principal and interest, unpaid after making any such application of payments as herein receipted shall be the interest bearing principal amount of this obligation for the next succeeding interest computation period. If any payment is not received within _____ (_____) days of payment date, there shall be a late charge of (_____ %) percent assessed.

The Vendees may pay the entire purchase price on this contract without prepayment penalty. The monthly installments shall be payable as directed by the Vendor herein.

2.   ENCUMBRANCES:
Said real estate is presently subject to a mortgage with_____ and the Vendor shall not place any additional mortgage on the premises without the prior written permission of the Vendees. To protect Vendee's interests.

Vendee may elect at any time to pay any sums due hereunder directly to the mortgagee, and any amounts remaining to the Vendor.

Vendor understands that this transaction may permit the mortgagee to exercise their right to accelerate the loan and to call the remaining balance due. In any such event, the Vendor agrees to hold Vendee harmless and in no way liable for any damage to Vendor because of such action. Vendor initials _____.

3.   EVIDENCE OF TITLE:
The Vendor shall be required to provide an abstract or guarantee of title, statement of title, title insurance, or such other evidence of title to Vendee's satisfaction.

4.   RECORDING OF CONTRACT:
The Vendor shall permit a copy of this contract to be recorded in the _____County Recorder's Office at Vendee's discretion at any time subsequent to the execution of this Contract by the parties hereto.

5.   REAL ESTATE TAXES:
Real estate taxes to the County Treasurer shall remain In the Vendor's name throughout the term of this agreement. Payment of said taxes shall be the responsibility of the Vendee upon the execution of this agreement, and [___] shall [___] shall not be escrowed and added to the payment required by Vendee herein.

6.   INSURANCE AND MAINTENANCE:
The Vendor shall insure the property with a non owner-occupant (landlord) policy against fire and extended coverage to the benefit of both parties as their Interests may appear herein. Said policy shall be for an amount no less than _____, payment of which shall be the responsibility of the Vendee, and which shall be escrowed and added to the payment due herein.

Vendees shall keep the building in a good state of repair at the Vendees expense. At such time as the Vendor inspects the premises and finds that repairs are necessary, Vendor shall request that these repairs be made within sixty (60) days at the Vendees expense.

Figure 7:3 Sample Form – Land Contract Agreement Page 2

The Vendees have inspected the premises constituting the subject matter of this Land Contract, and no representations have been made to the Vendee by the Vendor in regard to the condition of said premises: and it is agreed that the said premises are being sold to the Vendee as the same now exists and that the Vendor shall have no obligation to do or furnish anything toward the improvement of said premises.

Vendor shall furnish a clear termite report at Vendor's expense prior to executing this contract. If the property has live infestation of wood destroying insects, Vendor will pay costs of treatment and repair damages caused by same. If Vendor elects not to do so. Vendee may elect to waive Vendors responsibility and proceed. Vendee may elect not to proceed with this contract. Notice of each election shall be given in writing within five (5) days of receipt of Vendor of the notice of infestation and receipt by Vendee of Vendors notice as to intention to remedy.

7. POSSESSION
    The Vendee shall be given possession of the above described premises at Contract execution and shall thereafter have and hold the same subject to default provisions hereinafter set forth.

8. Delivery of DEED:
    Upon full payment of this contract, Vendor shall issue a General Warranty deed to the Vendees free of all encumbrances except as otherwise set forth. In addition, Vendees reserves the right to convert this contract into a note and mortgage which shall bear the same terms as the contract for the remaining balance, and receive a warranty Deed to Vendees or assigns from Vendor, anytime the following conditions have been met by then Vendees,

    1. At least 20% of the purchase price has been paid to the Vendor.
    2. Vendee is willing to pay all the costs of title transfer and document preparations.

9. DEFAULT BY VENDEES
    If an installment payment to be made by the Vendee under the terms of this Land Contract is not paid by the Vendee when due or within thirty (30) days thereafter, the entire unpaid balance shall become due and collectable at the election of the Vendor and the Vendor shall be entitled to all the remedies provided for by the laws of this state and/or to do any other remedies and/or seek relief now or hereafter provided for by law to such Vendor; and in the event of the breach of this contract in any other respect by the Vendee, Vendor shall be entitled to all relief now or hereinafter provided for by the laws of this state.

    Failure of Vendee to maintain current the status of all real estate taxes and insurance premiums as required herein shall permit Vendor the option to pay any such premiums, taxes, interest, or penalty (ies), and to add the amount paid to the principal amount owing under this contract, or to exercise any remedies available to the Vendor as per the preceding paragraph.

    Waiver by the Vendor of a default or a number of defaults in the performance hereof by the Vendee shall not be construed as a waiver of any future default no matter how similar.

10. GENERAL PROVISIONS:
    There are no known pending orders issued by any governmental authority with respect to this property other than those spelled out in this Land Contract prior to closing date for the execution of the contract.

11. SPECIAL PROVISIONS:

    _____
    _____
    _____

Figure 7:3 Sample Form – Land Contract Agreement Page 3

OPTION TO PURCHASE

The option to purchase real property is a contract under which the owner grants the right to purchase real property to another person at a specific price and within a specific period.

CREATION   Options may be created through various instruments including:

- Option in gross

- Mortgage

- Will

- Lease with an option clause

- Addenda to the lease

- Other documents established by state law

The existence of any of these instruments will require you to conduct additional research. You will need to establish if the option conveyed has expired in time. If the option offered has not expired in time you will need to determine if an additional document was created terminating the option offered. If neither of these items exist, then an exception in Schedule B of the title commitment and policy.

TERMINATION   To delete the exception to the option some or all of the following criteria must be met:

- Expiration of the option

- Compliance of the expiration with statutory law

- Release of the option by the optionee in an executed and recorded instrument

- Judicial determination of the option as invalid,

- The title underwriter may also issue an opinion as to the validity of the option and the need for a specific exception.

If an option agreement exists in the search record, you should note all of the details of each document in existence pertaining to that option and consult the title underwriter for a determination of the necessary processes to be followed.

OPTION AGREEMENT FOR PURCHASE OF REAL PROPERTY

THIS OPTION AGREEMENT ("Agreement") made and entered into this _____ day of _____, 20_____, by and between _____, whose principal address is _____, hereinafter referred to as "Seller" and _____, whose principal address is _____, hereinafter referred to as "Purchaser":

W I T N E S S E T H:

WHEREAS, Seller is the fee simple owner of certain real property being, lying and situated in the County of _____, State of _____, such real property having the street address of _____ ("Premises") and such property being more particularly described as follows: _____and,

WHEREAS, Purchaser desires to procure an option to purchase the Premises upon the terms and provisions as hereinafter set forth.

NOW, THEREFORE, for good and valuable consideration the receipt and sufficiency of which is hereby acknowledged by the parties hereto and for the mutual covenants contained herein, Seller and Purchaser hereby agree as follows:

1. DEFINITIONS For the purposes of this Agreement, the following terms shall have the following meanings:
    (a) "Execution Date" shall mean the day upon which the last party to this Agreement shall duly execute this Agreement
    (b) "Option Fee" shall mean the total sum of a down payment of _____ percent (___%) of the total purchase price of the Premises plus all closing costs, payable as set forth below;
    (c) "Option Term" shall mean that period of time commencing on the Execution Date and ending on or before _____, 20_____
    (d) "Option Exercise Date" shall mean that date, within the Option Term, upon which the Purchaser shall send its written notice to Seller exercising its Option to Purchase
    (e) "Closing Date" shall mean the last day of the closing term or such other date during the closing term selected by Purchaser.

2. GRANT OF OPTION. For and in consideration of the Option Fee payable to Seller as set forth herein, Seller does hereby grant to Purchaser the exclusive right and Option ("Option") to purchase the premises upon the terms and conditions as set forth herein.

3. PAYMENT OF OPTION FEE Purchaser agrees to pay the Seller a down payment of _____ percent (___%) of the total purchase price of the Premises plus all closing costs upon the Execution Date.

4. EXERCISE OF OPTION Purchaser may exercise its exclusive right to purchase the Premises pursuant to the Option, at any time during the Option Term, by giving written notice thereof to Seller. As provided for above, the date of sending of said notice shall be the Option Exercise Date. In the event the Purchaser does not exercise its exclusive right to purchase the Premises granted by the Option during the Option Term, Seller shall be entitled to retain the Option Fee, and this agreement shall become absolutely null and void and neither party hereto shall have any other liability, obligation, or duty herein under or pursuant to this Agreement.

5. CONTRACT FOR PURCHASE & SALE OF REAL PROPERTY

Figure 7:5 Sample Form – Option Agreement Page

In the event that the Purchaser exercises its exclusive Option as provided for in the preceding paragraph, Seller agrees to sell, Purchaser agrees to buy the Premises, and both parties agree to execute a contract for such purchase and sale of the Premises in accordance with the following terms and conditions:

(a) Purchase Price. The purchase price for the Premises shall be the sum of _____ ($_____); however, Purchaser shall receive a credit toward such purchase price in the amount of the Option Fee thus, Purchaser shall pay to Seller at closing the sum of _____ ($_____);

(b) Closing Date. The closing date shall be on _____, 20____ or at any other date during the Option Term as may be selected by Purchaser

(c) Closing Costs Purchaser's and Seller's costs of closing the Contract shall be borne by Purchase and shall be prepaid as a portion of the Option Fee;

(d) Default by Purchaser; Remedies of Seller. In the event Purchaser, after exercise of the Option, fails to proceed with the closing of the purchase of the Premises pursuant to the terms and provisions as contained herein and/or under the Contract, Seller shall be entitled to retain the Option Fee as liquidated damages and shall have no further recourse against Purchaser;

(e) Default by Seller; Remedies of Purchaser. In the event Seller fails to close the sale of the Premises pursuant to the terms and provisions of this Agreement and/or under the Contract, Purchaser shall be entitled to either sue for specific performance of the real estate purchase and sale contract or terminate such Contract and sue for money damages.

6. MISCELLANEOUS

(a) Execution by Both Parties This Agreement shall not become effective and binding until fully executed by both Purchaser and Seller.

(b) Notice: All notices, demands, and/or consents provided for in this Agreement shall be in writing and shall be delivered to the parties hereto by hand or by United States Mail with postage pre-paid. Such notices shall be deemed to have been served on the date mailed, postage pre-paid. All such notices and communications shall be addressed to the Seller at _____ and to Purchaser at _____ or at such other address as either may specify to the other in writing.

(c) Fee Governing Law This Agreement shall be governed by and construed in accordance with the laws of the State of _____.

(d) Successors and Assigns This Agreement shall apply to, inure to the benefit of, and be binding upon and enforceable against the parties hereto and their respective heirs, successors, and or assigns, to the extent as if specified at length throughout this Agreement.

(e) Time: Time is of the essence of this Agreement.

(f) Headings The headings inserted at the beginning of each paragraph and/or subparagraph are for convenience of reference only and shall not limit or otherwise affect or be used in the construction of any terms or provisions hereof.

(g) Cost of this Agreement: Any cost and/or fees incurred by the Purchaser or Seller in executing this Agreement shall be borne by the respective party incurring such cost and/or fee.

(h) Entire Agreement This Agreement contains all of the terms, promises, covenants, conditions and representations made or entered into by or between Seller and Purchaser and supersedes all prior discussions and agreements whether written or oral between Seller and Purchaser with respect to the Option and all other matters contained herein and constitutes the sole and entire agreement between Seller and Purchaser with respect thereto. This Agreement may not be modified or amended unless such amendment is set forth in writing and executed by both Seller and Purchaser with the formalities hereof.

IN WITNESS WHEREOF, the parties hereto have caused this Agreement to be executed under proper authority:
As to Purchaser this _____ day of _____, 20_____

Figure 7:7 Sample Form – Option Agreement Page 2

This form is included for example purposes only. The form is modified from the acceptable real estate forms as released by HUD. The services of a real estate professional should be retained to ensure the correct forms are used for your transaction.

Agreement to Lease with Option to Purchase

Parties:

Buyer _____ of _____

and

Seller_____ of_____

In consideration of the payments, covenants, agreements and conditions herein contained the above parties hereby agree to lease with an option the following property:

Subject: Property Address:_____

Legal Description: _____

_____

Personal Property _____

Personal property to be transferred at closing by bill of sale free of any encumbrances.

Existing Loans- At time of closing buyer may elect to take title subject to the existing loans to_____

In the amount of $_____ bearing interest rate of _____% payable _____ (P&I)

Or the loan will be paid off by the seller.

Loan Number_____ Date last payment made_____

Other Liens, back taxes, etc._____

Term of lease and option _____months beginning _____

Monthly Payment $_____due on the _____day of each month beginning_____ 20____

Monthly credit toward purchase price when rent paid on time $_____

Purchase Price $_____, additional option consideration _____to apply towards purchase price.

1. TERMS: Seller agrees that upon the exercise of the option they will assist in financing by taking as part of the purchase price a note in the amount of $_____ with payments of $_____ beginning _____.
2. MAINTENANCE: The buyers shall pay for all repairs costing less than $ 100.00 each month. Repairs costing $100 or more will be paid by the owner. Should the owner fail to make repairs to maintain the house in its current condition, the buyer may have said repairs made and receive a credit equal to 200% of the cost of the repair toward the purchase price and a full credit toward the next payment due.
3. SELLERS AGREEMENT NOT TO FURTHER ENCUMBER: Sellers agree not to refinance the property, nor to modify any existing loans, nor to transfer any interest in the property during the term of this agreement.
4. PAYMENTS ON EXISTING LOANS, TAXES AND INSURANCE: Seller shall be responsible for paying the taxes, loan payments and for keeping the property insured for its full replacement value during the term of this agreement. In the event seller fails to make payments when due of taxes, insurance, or loan payments, buyer may elect to make said pays due payments and receive 200% of their amount credited toward the purchase price and full credit toward the next payment due the seller.
5. PRO RATA: Taxes, insurance, and loan interest shall be prorated as of the date of closing of the purchase.
6. BUYER & SELLER: agree to fully execute and place in escrow with _____ instruments needed to convey title. The seller shall deposit and executed warranty deed, and copies of existing mortgages, notes, title insurance policies, and surveys. Buyer shall deposit an executed quitclaim

Figure 7:8 Sample Form – Lease Option Agreement Page 1

deed that will be delivered to the seller in the event of default by the buyer under this contract. All agree to sign an escrow agreement that will empower the escrow agent to close the transaction if all terms of the contract are met, and that will hold the agent harmless.

7. TRANSFER OF TITLE: In the event buyer chooses to exercise their option to purchase, they will notify the seller during the term of this agreement. Within 15 days of receipt of such notice, sellers agree to convey good and marketable title, free from all encumbrances except those that a buyer wishes to take title subject to. Sellers further agree to furnish an owner's title binder within 5 days after receiving notice, showing no exceptions other than as listed above, and furnish a policy of title insurance at closing.

8. DAMAGES: In the event seller fails to perform, buyer will be entitled to recover all monies paid on this agreement, and may pursue all other legal remedies available. Seller will be responsible for all costs including a reasonable attorney's fee. In the event buyer fails to exercise the option, all option consideration, and rents paid will be forfeited as full-liquidated damages.

9. RECORDING: All parties agree that this agreement or a memorandum including any parts of their agreement acceptable to the buyer may be recorded.

10. SUCCESSORS AND ASSIGNS & SUBLETTING: The terms and conditions of this contract shall bind all successors, heirs, administrators, executors, assigns, and those subletting.

11. ACCESS AND ADVERTISING: Sellers agree that the buyer may advertise the property and shall immediately have access during reasonable hours to show the property to others.

12. TIME IS OF THE ESSENCE IN ALL MATTERS OF THE AGREEMENT

13. OTHER TERMS:

_____
_____
_____
_____
_____

The undersigned agree to buy and sell on the above terms, have-read, fully understand and verify the above information as being correct. All parties acknowledge that this is a legally binding contract and are advised to seek the counsel of an attorney.

Seller: _____   Date: _____

Seller: _____   Date: _____

Buyer _____   Date: _____

Buyer _____   Date: _____

State of _____   County of _____

Figure 7:9 Sample Form – Lease Option Agreement Page 2

This form is included for example purposes only. The form is modified from the acceptable real estate forms as released by HUD. The services of a real estate professional should be retained to ensure the correct forms are used for your transaction.

The contracts listed are not the only transfer documents you may encounter during your search activity. These are included because of the commonality with which they are used.

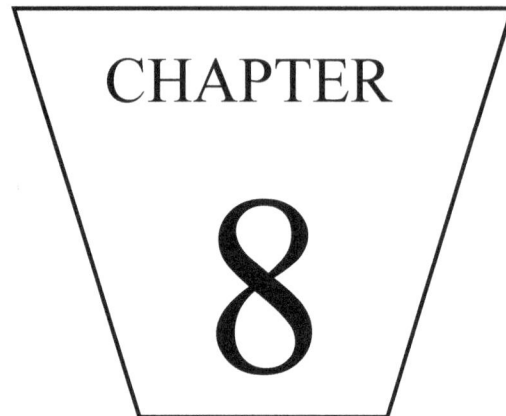

CHAPTER

8

CONDUCTING THE SEARCH

The chapters leading to this one have been preparing you for entrance into the public records room to conduct a search into the property. Now that you have gained the background you will need, it is time to gain a better understanding of the layout of the public records system. This understanding will assist you in implementing what you have learned to conduct the valuable research that will enable the transfer of real property.

N ow that you have gained a solid foundation in the fundamentals of real estate, you must gain an understanding of how this knowledge will be applied to your abstracting career.

Each element of the training you have studied lends itself to a stronger understanding of the items you will research within the pubic records. Before entering the public records to begin the second phase of this training program, you must understand the history behind the keeping of records in a centralized location and the methods of organizing those records.

Until the enactment of the statute frauds in England and 1677, determination regarding ownership of a parcel of land was usually a matter of simply observing who was in physical possession of the land. A landowner would provide notice to the world that he claimed ownership of a parcel of land by visibly occupying his land.

After 1677, Britain required recorded deeds to show transfers of ownership. Today, both research of the records and visible observance of the land are needed to ensure adequate knowledge of who is claiming ownership interest in a piece of property.

Two methods might be employed to give notice of a claim or right to land.

- One is the recorded document in the public records system to give notice to that effect.

- The other is by visibly occupying or otherwise making use of the land.

The law holds interested parties responsible for examining the public records system and looking at the land for this notice of prior claim.

Your function is to conduct the applicable research into the public records.

Constructive Notice Constructive notice is also sometimes referred to as legal notice.

Constructive notice is accomplished by the recording of a document at the county recorder office. Recording the notice

- Provides notice to the public of the documents existence and contents.

- Charges the public with the responsibility of looking into the public records and at the property itself to obtain all the knowledge necessary concerning who claims interest in a piece of land.

The fundamental purpose of the abstracting activity is to review all items that indicate constructive notice and provide the details of these recorded documents.

Constructive notice may also be accomplished by visibly occupying the property.

It will typically not be a portion of your job duties to observe the land being researched to determine if an individual is visibly occupying the land.

Inquiry notice A person interested in a property is responsible for making inquiry beyond the public records to determine if anyone is giving visible notice to interest in the land.

When dealing with inquiry notice, the law presumes a reasonably diligent person will obtain information by making further inquiry into the ownership of the property.

Actual Notice   Actual notice is the knowledge that one has actually gained based on what is:

> Seen

> Heard

> Read

> Observed

> Witnessed

- If you read a deed stating transfer occurred from Smith to Jones, you have obtained actual notice of the deed and that Smith's claim to the property has been transferred to Jones.

- If the interested party goes to the property and sees someone has possession, that person has actual notice that the people claiming to be there are present.

Remember that anyone claiming an interest or right to the use of a piece of land is expected to make it known by either recorded claim or visible use of the property.

Anyone acquiring an interest in the property is expected to look at the public records system to determine if anyone is making a claim against property and to make visual inspection to determine if anyone is making claim to the property through use.

Part of your job as an abstractor will be to scrutinize the public records to determine what claims are held against the land.

It is vital that abstractors have a through knowledge of the public records system and recording practices in the area in which they conduct searches. All states have recording acts, which govern the processes of the recording of documents pertaining to the transfer of real estate. These documents are typically placed on file at the Recorder of Deeds office in the county courthouse that governs the region in which the property is located.

Some of the documents, which you may review during a search of the public records system, include:

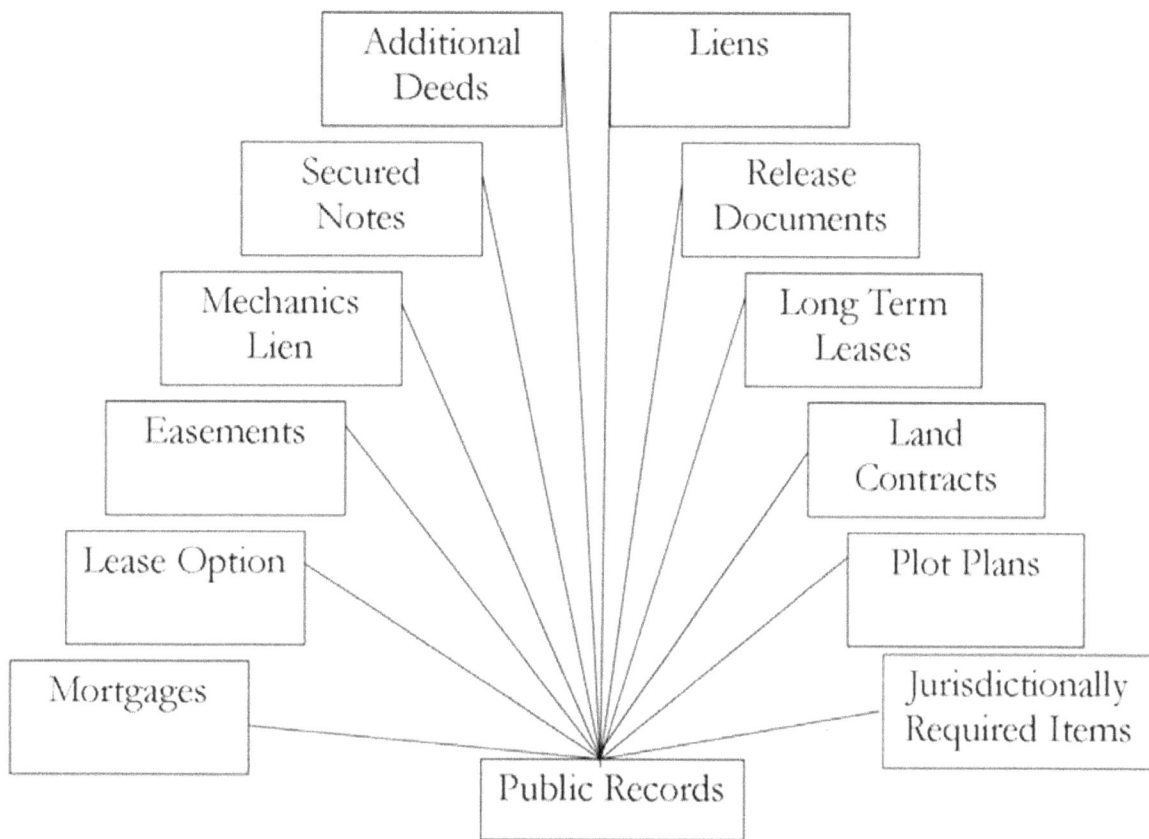

Figure 8:1 Diagram – Public Records System

The documents recorded within the public records system are done so in a chronological order. This time-based order enables the chain of title to be sufficiently researched backward through time. Each document within the records system will contain a stamp indicating the date and time of recording and be designated by a book location and page number.

- The documents presented for recording will be photocopied and the copies will be placed in the book with indexes.

  The book and index placement will be noted on the document.

  The indexes may take a variety of forms that will be discussed later in this chapter.

- The original copy of the recorded instrument will be returned to the owner for their records.

A through examination of these records allows you to determine what actions previous owners may have taken that effect the rights and interest in the property. The results of this examination are also termed determining the quality of the title. In other words, it will show you the condition of the title during the current ownership as well as under previous owners.

When completing an abstract of title you will begin with the most recently recorded document and work backwards through the public records system until you reach the original land grant pertaining to the real property being researched. Most of the documents you review will refer to the prior document in the history that should be reviewed. Some documents such as a divorce decree will require that you research by individual to determine additional information rather than by property. Individuals or entities that hold an interest can encumber property in a variety of methods. We have provided you with the documents pertaining to the possible encumbrances you must research with regard to each individual named as an interested party throughout the chain of title.

All States have recording acts that provide guidelines for the recording of every instrument or document. This recordation notifies all interested parties of any interest or right in land that has been created, transferred, or encumbered.

- Within each state, each county has an office known at the county recorder's office. These can also be termed the public recorder's office, county clerk's office, circuit court clerk's office, county registrar's office, or bureau of conveyances.

- The person in charge of these offices is called the recorder, clerk, or registrar.

- These offices are frequently located within the county governmental offices.

- Each public recorder's office records all documents that are submitted pertaining to real property in that particular county.

- Anyone seeking information regarding ownership of land in a particular county would go to that recorder's office.

- Some cities also maintain a record room where documents are recorded.

- Recording acts permit the recording of any estate, rights, claim, or interest in land.

- Lesser rights are often not recorded because of the costs and effort involved. Rental agreements and leases for a year or less fall into this category of leaser rights.

- Each document brought to the public recorder's office for recordation is photocopied and returned to the original owner.

- The photocopies are placed in chronological order with the copies of other documents.

- These are stamped with consecutive page numbers and bound into a book.

- These books are then placed in chronological order and shelved in a location open to the public for inspection.

Binding documents in chronological order is necessary to establish the chronological priority of documents.

DOCUMENT INDEXES

The act of binding documents in chronological order does assist in establishing the priority of all matters affecting a parcel of land, however it does not provide for an easy method of research relative to the land. Indexes have been created to assist the searcher in determining what records exist ore locating each record applicable to a specific parcel of land or the owner of record.

The most commonly used indexes are the grantor and the grantee indexes. Some states use tract indexes.

TRACT INDEX The tract index is the simplest to use when one is attempting to locate all records applicable to a specific parcel of land.

The tract index allocates one page to listing all of the recorded items pertaining to a single parcel of land.

- The page will provide a listing of all recorded deeds mortgages and other documents that relate to that parcel.

- A few words describing each document will be provided.

- The book and page number where a photocopy of the document will be entered.

If you are conducting research in a State that uses this type of index, you will find your work is greatly reduced. These indexes make researching documents pertaining to a particular parcel an easier process. You must remember though, that actions taken by owners and not designated to a specific parcel may also affect the property you are researching. A search beyond those items listed in this index and into owner-specific records may be needed.

GRANTOR INDEX/
GRANTEE INDEX Grantor and grantee indexes are alphabetical indexes created yearly and bound in book form.

The basic principal of the Grantee and Grantor Indexes used are the same though the actual appearance of the indexes may vary by jurisdiction.

A grantor index lists all grantors named in documents recorded during a specified year in alphabetical order.

- The grantors are named

- The grantee is named

- The book and page where the photocopied document can be found is listed

- A few words describing the document is entered

The grantee contains the same essential information as the grantor index but the arrangement of the entries is by grantee name.

To use the grantee or grantor index to search public records, you would locate the record for the property owner who has or had an interest in the property being researched.

You would then refer to the specified documents listed under the name of that owner.

- Each of these documents will provide you with information pertinent to your research.

- You will also use these documents to locate the name of the owner from whom the current owner took possession.

You will then repeat the processes for each owner listed on any document pertinent to the parcel you are researching.

The process will continue backward through time until you have located all matters pertinent to the property.

This process of moving backward and noting every grantor and grantee listed within the document assists you to create a chain of title.

- You should view the chain of title as a group of links moving backward through time.

- If a link is missing from the chain, the connection from the present day to the original grant of the land is not complete.

  The indexes are meant to provide you with the necessary directions to complete this chain.

  If an item exists that breaks the chain, you may need to refer to other indexes, records or areas to mend the break in the chain.

You will use the chain created through your research to assist you in determining any actions that an owner of the property you are researching may have taken to encumber the land. It is important to remember that you must research every owner listed in relationship to the parcel so that you can locate any activity that might affect the value or use of the property.

There are clues to the depth of research that will be necessary within the documents you review. Specific deeds will provide specific assurance of the status of the title when the deed was created. These deeds may also contain warranties and covenants that will show you the status of the title before the date of the deed. By gaining an understanding of the implications of each deed and the impact the deed may have on the property, you may limit the work investment required during your research portion. The chapter following this one will provide you with an insight into the potential deeds you might encounter during your search, the inclusions of these deeds and the implications of the different deeds that might exist.

PENDING LAWSUITS AND JUDGMENTS

In addition to the other matters you will research, you should make inquiry to determine if there are any pending lawsuits or judgments affecting the title you are searching.

LIS PENDENS INDEX

Most public records contain an additional index known as the Lis Pendens Index. This index will detail pending and unresolved lawsuits within the county that the recorders office serves. You will be interested in any lawsuit that might affect the title or ownership of the property.

You will search the records referenced in this index for any action that relates to any owner of the property you are researching.

Example: A divorce of a married couple who owned the property is shown within the Lis Pendens index.

The divorce decree issued following the proceedings dictates that only one individual shall hold title to the property in the future.

You must search all records applicable to that property prior to the issuance of the divorce decree that relate to both property owners but may search records following the divorce decree that apply to the partner granted the ownership through the decree.

GENERAL EXECUTION DOCKET

The General Execution Docket can also provide vital insight into the possible items that might make proving marketable title an issue. This docket shows a detail of judgments entered against an individual.

If an individual who is listed as having ownership interest in the property title you are researching has a judgment entered within the general execution docket, you must note the specifics and conduct further research to determine if a satisfactory resolution has been made of if the judgment might affect the ownership interest of the property title you are researching.

Specifics pertaining to the types of judgments that may exist and the methods of application and termination you should locate for each judgment are included in the previous chapters. You should gain a comprehensive understanding of the methodology for handling judgments so that you can adequately research the records applicable to the property you are researching

AD VALOREM DOCKET

You will wish to confirm the amount of all taxes assessed against the property as well as the status of payment of these taxes. At times, an owner will fail to pay the real estate property taxes assessed against the property. These past-due tax assessments must be paid in full prior to the transfer of the real property title. You must confirm the tax payment history and any judgments for past due taxes that may exist against the property.

The Ad Valorem Docket will provide a specific listing of all tax assessments that have been reduced to a judgment against the property. Tax Assessment Judgments are liens against a specific property and as such must be addressed.

The Tax Assessor will be able to supply you with the current tax bill totals and payment due dates.

You should incorporate all tax matters into the abstracting summary.

CHAPTER

9

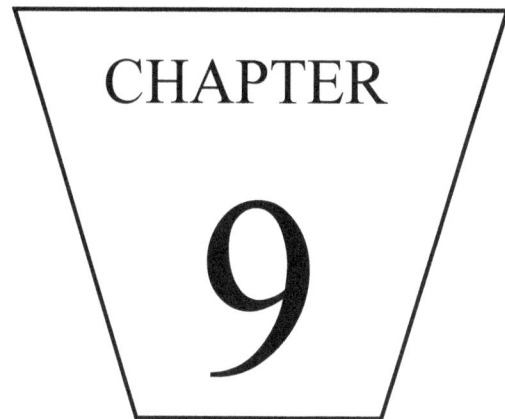

THE TITLE EXAM

The title examination researches and reports on four basic items.

- Chain of Title

- Breaks in the Chain of Title

- Defects in the Chain of Title

- Status of Defects in the Chain of Title

Chain of Title

The chain of title is a record that links together all previous owners of a property and includes any actions that affected the title during the terms of ownership.

The chain is arranged consecutively from the initial government patent or original source of the title to the present titleholder.

```
┌──────────────────────────────────┐
│ United States Government          │
│ To John Doe                       │
│ By Homestead Act                  │
│ Recorded 01/01/1855               │
│ Book 7, page 1                    │
│                                   │
└──────────────────────────────────┘
                 │
                 ▼
┌──────────────────────────────────┐
│ John Doe                          │
│ To Joe Smith and Spouse Jane      │
│ By Warranty Deed                  │
│ Recorded 01/17/1899               │
│ Book 30, page 44                  │
│                                   │
└──────────────────────────────────┘
                 │
                 ▼
┌──────────────────────────────────┐
│ Joe Smith dies on                 │
│ 06/05/1939                        │
│ Spouse Jane Smith dies            │
│ On 12/28/1944                     │
│                                   │
│                                   │
└──────────────────────────────────┘
                 │
                 ▼
┌──────────────────────────────────┐
│ Jerry Lawyer, executor of the     │
│ estate of Joe Smith and spouse    │
│ Jane Smith to                     │
│ Child Smith                       │
│ By will                           │
│ Probated 07/01/1945               │
└──────────────────────────────────┘
                 │
                 ▼
┌──────────────────────────────────┐
│ Child Smith                       │
│ To Steven Doe                     │
│ By Warranty Deed                  │
│ Recorded 11/21/1982               │
│ Book 2715, page 785               │
│                                   │
└──────────────────────────────────┘
```

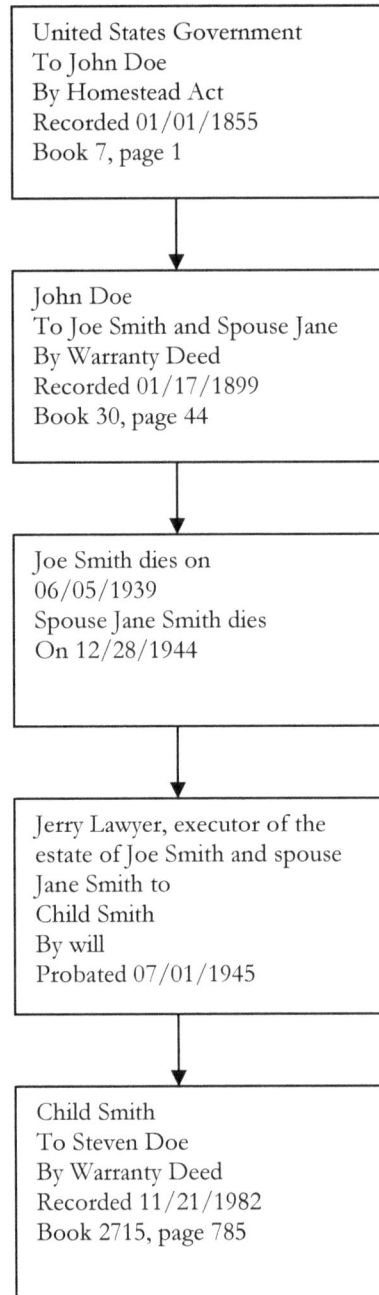

Figure 9:1 Diagram – Chain of Title

The chain of title will include a compilation of all real estate instruments and other matters of record that affect the title of a particular piece of land.

You should view the chain of title as the linkage of property ownership to connect the present owner to the original source of the title.

In most cases, the chain starts at the original sale or grant of the land from the government to a private citizen.

Breaks in the Chain of Title

At times, a break may occur in the chain of title. These breaks occur for a variety of reasons including

- Missing deeds of conveyance

- Insufficient deeds of conveyance or other instruments

- Lack of adequate judicial proceedings

- Judicial determinations that are not filed for record at the office designated by statute

- Factual or non-judicial information that was not filed for record at the office designated by statute

- Other reasons as statutorily proscribed

When a break in the chain of title occurs, it must be remedied. This can be accomplished by

- The implementation and completion of the proper judicial proceedings

- Filing for record certified copies of judicial decrees or determinations that were previously not filed in the proper office designated by statute.

- Obtaining deeds of conveyance or suitable instruments from the interested parties and filing them for record in the office designated by statute.

- Obtaining affidavits, statements or declarations reciting the existence factual situations or events that are filed for record in the real estate records office designated by statute

- Locating a document or previous action taken that remedies the break in the chain of title

    The last item is one that can be accomplished by the title abstractor and an attempt to complete the location actions should be made before any other action on the remedy list is attempted. To accomplish this location and regain the title sequence a search outside the recorder's office may be needed.

Example 1: The grantor's administrator or executor may not have properly followed the statute when the owner died.

Example 2: A mortgage may have been foreclosed against the property and require additional searching to verify the validity of all actions taken.

Example 3: A judicial or ministerial sale may have occurred in the chain. This requires additional research to determine if the sale was conducted in compliance with all applicable regulations and statutes.

To regain the title chain and attempt to remove the matter that places the interest of the owner of the property at risk, you expand your search activity.

Remedy 1: Probate records will provide you with the actions taken and the ownership interest transferred at the time that an owner dies.

Remedy 2: Civil court actions and records will provide you with the details of actions of foreclosure and the resulting transfer of ownership.

Remedy 3: Ad Valorem records and the location of the applicable tax deed will provide you with a new title chain resulting from a tax sale action by the courts.

You must complete the entire process of compiling a chain of title. Any time you come to an apparent break in the chain of title, you must determine what records you will need to review to regain the chain and complete the research process.

The chain of title is complete when all events are documented from the original source of title to the present owner. If there is a missing link, the current owner does not have valid title to the property.

Defect in Title

In addition to constructing the specific chain of title, you must determine what defects in the title exist. A defect in the title would include any item recorded against the title that has not apparently been terminated or that limits the rights of the property owner to make full use of their land and enjoy the full bundle of rights. These might include

- Mortgages

- Liens

- Judgments

- Easements

- Condemnation

- Lawsuits

- Active contracts

- Boundary Line Agreements

Any defect located within the chain of the title that is not removed through a subsequently recorded instrument must be detailed within the abstractor summary. The following pages will provide you with a guideline that will assist you in locating the records that must be incorporated into your abstracting summary.

Status of Defect

Once a defect is identified, the status of that defect must be determined.

- The defect may still exist against the title. If the defect still exists, you must make careful notations regarding the recorded instruments pertaining to the defect so the title underwriter may make a competent decision regarding further actions that will be taken.

- The defect may have been changed or altered. If a defect exists, you will have made careful notations. Any change or alteration to the defect should also be detailed so that the most applicable wording can be used to except the defect.

- The defect may have been eliminated. If a defect that once existed has been eliminated, you should make additional notations regarding the method, time and process followed during the elimination. This enables the title underwriter to confirm that the defect has been properly removed from the chain of title, determine additional removal actions that may be needed or word the exception with regard to the defect.

The goal of your research activity is to determine if the property you are researching offers a marketable title. A marketable title is on in which the current owner of the property can provide a valid and supportable transfer of the title to the property in the open market. To be considered marketable, the title must be shown to be a good, viable title free of liens and other defects.

A secondary goal as the title abstractor will be to research the title to determine if title insurance can be issued with no specific exceptions to coverage. An exception, as you have learned, is an item for which the title underwriter feels coverage cannot be provided. These exceptions may include any item described in the training you have reviewed thus far as well as any additional or unusual matter that you discover during your search that places the interest of the purchasing party at risk.

The following quick list will assist you in locating the necessary records to complete the abstract of the title, locate any defects that exist and determine the status of any defects that exist within the chain of the title you are researching.

- **Grantee/Grantor Indexes**

  ➢ Current Property Owner

  This entry will be located in the index for the year that the current owner obtained his interest in the property.

  The index will provide a reference to the book and page where the deed of conveyance by which he took title to the property is recorded.

  ➢ Previous Owner

  A review of the deed of conveyance will provide you with the name of the owner from whom the current owner took possession. You will then work backward through the previous indexes to locate the entry that indicates the document by which this previous owner took ownership interest.

  By continuing this process backward through all deeds of conveyance, you will construct the chain of title.

- **Grantor / Grantee Index / Mortgagee Index**

  ➢ Real property transfer documents

  ➢ Liens

  ➢ Judgments

  ➢ Assignments

  ➢ Power of attorney

  ➢ Additional Contracts

  ➢ Other matters pertaining to the specific title you are researching

Some states will place mortgages within the general grantor and grantee indexes, while others will have ea separate index that details only mortgage instruments. You must determine the method employed in the state where you will conduct your research.

If a mortgage is located within the public records, the applicable records will provide you with the status of the mortgage. The mortgage may be satisfied, release or active. If a mortgage is released and satisfied, the recorder's office will place a note on the margin of the recorded mortgage instrument indicating the book and page where the release is located.

- **Judgment Rolls, Lis Pendens Index, General Execution Docket**

  ➤ General Liens

  ➤ Specific Liens

  ➤ Pending Lawsuits

A defect on the title may exist in the form of a judgment or pending lawsuits may affect the transfer of ownership interest. You can locate information pertaining to judgments within the Judgment Rolls and relating to pending lawsuits within the Lis Pendens Index.

- **Assessor's Records / Ad Valorem Docket**

  ➤ Current property taxes

  ➤ Delinquent Taxes

  ➤ Special Assessments

  ➤ Tax Liens

  ➤ Current owner name and address

- **County map records, survey reports and plat maps**

  ➤ Legal Description

  ➤ Property size

  ➤ Boundary specifics

- ➤ Boundary Line Issues or Agreements

- ➤ Appurtenances

- ➤ Easements

- ➤ Right of Ways

- ➤ Right of Access

- ➤ Quality of Access

- ➤ Abutting or adjoining property and roads

- ➤ Measurements

- ➤ Improvements

- ➤ Easements

- ➤ Utilities

- ➤ Features

- ➤ Accretion or Erosion that alters the land description

- ➤ Littoral, riparian, beach rights

- ➤ Flood Plain Designation

- **Tract Index**

  - ➤ Real property transfer documents

  - ➤ Liens

  - ➤ Judgments

  - ➤ Assignments

  - ➤ Power of attorney

  - ➤ Additional Contracts

➤ Other matters pertaining to the specific title you are researching

- **Civil court records**

  ➤ Foreclosure actions

  ➤ Legal Proceedings against a property owner

  ➤ Other legal proceedings

- **Divorce Records**

  ➤ To locate the removal of a property owner's interest through a divorce decree

- **Marriage Records**

  ➤ To determine the addition of a potential property owner through a marriage

- **Probate court records**

  ➤ Additional interest transfers

  ➤ Status of inheritance and estate tax payments

- **State and Federal tax lien logs**

  ➤ To aid in the determination of whether any federal or state liens against a property owner may have attached to the property

ABSTRACTING SUMMARY

As we explained previously, the chain of title is the linking of each owner, from the original land grant to the present owner. In establishing the chain of title, you must begin with the current owner and work backward in time. You will research the records to determine if the current owner received a valid title from the prior owner. You will continue this process backward in time, confirming the status or marketability of the title received by each subsequent owner from the prior owner.

The determination of the status of the title includes the research you have been hired to conduct. Any individual, with little training, can review deed documents and other transfer records to gain information as to the specifics of each owner of a parcel. You must also gather information regarding the mortgages, liens, encumbrances, easements, and other matters we have described in the previous Chapters, as they existed at any point in the chain of title.

A sample abstracting form is included for your review. This form is a sample of the type of form you will encounter within the industry. You should familiarize yourself with the inclusions, but be aware that the forms used by different offices and within different regions will vary from the sample provided.

One form should be completed for each transfer and each owner of record discovered in relationship to the property you are researching. One form should also be generated for any matter that comes to your attention that is in excess of those items addressed on the form. For instance, if you locate information that indicates multiple mortgages are or were in existence, you may need to complete additional forms to adequately address the history.

You will note that the form does not include every possible contingency we have discussed. The proper completion of this form is one reason that the fundamentals of real estate as it applies to title research are vital to your success. The most common items of research will be included on an abstracting form. You should remember you might encounter many other situations and variations within the records system. You must ensure that you review any item that may affect the rights of the property owner. The note section is the location for you to put your knowledge base and research skills to use.

- You will review the most common items of research, entering the necessary information within the form.

- You will also review any questionable and unusual item that comes to your attention during the search.

  The specifics of these less common items of possible issues should be entered into the note area of your abstracting form.

- At times, you will encounter an item that requires the completion of an addendum to the form.

  You should provide as much information as possible to the title underwriter so that they may make a valid determination as to the condition and insurability of the title.

Hennin

SAMPLE ABSTRACTOR SUMMARY

Date: _____ Client: _____

Search Purpose/Notes: _____

Property Street Address: _____

Map Book Number: _____ Map Parcel Number: _____ Taxes: $_____/_____Status: _____

Grantor: _____ Grantee: _____

Deed Book Volume: _____ Page Number: _____ Date: _____ Deed Type: _____

Legal Description: _____
_____
_____

Access: _____

Easements/Restrictions/Other Matters: _____
_____

Mortgage: _____ Satisfied: Y/N Book / Page: _____/_____

Borrower(s) Name: _____

Notes: _____

Liens/Judgments/Other Matters: _____

Notes: _____

_____
_____
_____
_____
_____
_____

Figure 9:2 Sample Form – Abstractor Summary

ABSTRACTOR SUMMARY QUICK LIST

The abstract recites, in chronological order, all recorded

- Conveyances
- Easements
- Mortgages
- Wills
- Tax liens
- Agreements
- Judgments
- Pending lawsuits
- Marriages
- Divorces
- Deaths

And other items that might affect the title

The abstractor will:

- Summarize each document

- Note the book and page where the document may be found.

- Note the date was the document was recorded or entered

Example: When locating a deed:

- You will identify the grantor and grantee.

- You will note type of deed.

- You will note the warranties and covenants included in the deed.

- You will give a brief description of the property.

- You will list any conditions are restrictions found in the deed.

- You will detail the date on the deed and the recording date.

- You will note the book and page were the deed is recorded.

Example: In the case of a mortgage:

> You will list the borrower(s) full names.

> You will note the name of the lender.

> You will give a brief description of the mortgage contents.

> You will note if the mortgage has been repaid and satisfied.

> You will record the book and page location of the mortgage release document.

> You will note the date of recordation.

In some parts of the United States, the certified abstract is so valuable it is brought up-to-date each time the property sold.

Despite the diligent efforts of abstractors and attorneys to give an accurate picture of land ownership, there is no guarantee that the finished abstract or certificates are completely accurate.

The records system is complicated and occasionally documents may exist that do not come to light during the search.

Persons preparing abstract opinions are liable for mistakes due to their own negligence, and they can be sued for negligence that results in loss to the client. To be considered negligent you must have knowingly performed your search in a poor or haphazard manner. At times, the fault for an error may not be the responsibility of the abstractor.

Documents may not have been and therefore cannot be reviewed

The recorded deed in the title chain might be a forgery or invalid.

Example: If a married person represents himself on the deed as a single person, the deed may be invalidated.

A minor might have executed the deed causing potential validity   questions.

An incompetent person may have executed the deed causing the validity of the deed to be called into question.

The deed may contain erroneous descriptions.

Several other situations may exist that will create a defect that is not the discovered but is not due to the negligence of the abstractor.

- These situations often result in a substantial cost to the property owner.

- The fault might not lie with the abstractor or the attorney.

- The record office is not responsible for verifying contents of the deed.

To protect against the issues that may arise through no fault of the involved parties, organizations of private companies have been formed to sell insurance against losses. This insurance protects against losses arising from title defects such as these as well as from errors in the title examination.

TITLE INSURANCE

Initially title insurance was created for the benefit of attorneys who wanted protection from errors that they might make in the interpretation of an abstract. As time progressed, title insurance, also called a title guarantee, became available to anyone wishing to purchase it.

The basic principle of title insurance is similar to any form insurance. Many people pay a small amount into an insurance pool that is then available to anyone to cover a loss.

In some parts of the United States is customary to purchase the title insurance policy from an attorney who reads and certifies the abstract. Elsewhere is customary to purchase the insurance from a title company that combines the search and policy in one fee.

Process Overview

- When an abstractor receives a request for a title search, the first step that they will take is to examine the public records pertaining to the real property whose title status is being requested.

- Upon completion of the examination, the abstractor will submit the report to the attorney or title underwriter.

- The company attorney or title underwriter reviews the findings and issues an opinion as to the deed of the property.

- The attorney or title underwriter lists anyone else with the legitimate ownership interest in the property.

This additional listing may cause additional research requirements of the title abstractor.

- This information becomes the title report.

  Sometimes called a preliminary to the title report this is not a commitment by the title company to either insure the property.

  It does serve as the basis for a commitment to insure and is sometimes call a binder.

An abstract is the chronologically order or summary of all recorded events that affect the title to a given parcels land.

A title report is more like a snapshot that shows the condition of the title as specific noted time.

The title examination researches three basic components, which will then become the basis of each subsequent action in the title commitment and insurance process.

- Any defects in the title will be noted.

  Defects are found when the abstractor scrutinizes all actions to locate any record relating to any owner that may limit the rights of the individual taking ownership to the

  These defects could include unpaid mortgages, unpaid liens, easements, lawsuits, or other items that may effect or encumber the property being transferred.

- The status of the defects is determined.

  This means that, once a defect is found, the outcome of the defect will be researched.

- Title insurance will be issued confirming the status of the title.

  Title insurance is an insurance policy against any defects in the title that have not been specifically excluded from the insurance coverage.

  To exclude a specific item it will be named within the policy or policy addenda.

  The items named as exclusions will be those items located and specifically named by the abstractor researching the title.

  A primary focus of your position is to locate these potential exclusions.

- Title insurance policies may be issued to protect both the new owner and any lender named on the policy.

- Unlike many insurance policies that insure against future occurrences, title insurance will insure the condition of the title from the date of acquiring the insurance into the past.

- The title insurance policy will be based on the information remitted by the abstractor because of their research into the public records.

- Title insurance is typically issued for a one-time premium payment.

- If a title insurance policy has been issued on the property within the last 10 years, the search may be more limited and the liability incurred by the insurance company may be minimized.

    The buyer of the policy may receive a reduced rate as a result.

    This reduced rate is also called a reissue rate.

ISSUANCE

The Title Insurance Company will begin the process of creating the title insurance commitment by reviewing the inclusions of the abstracting summary you remit.

From this abstract, they will identify any legitimate defects that you have discovered during your research.

    A legitimate defect could be any of the items of research you unearthed, which limit the owner's fee simple rights in the property.

These defects are then noted on the title report.

    This title report is issued to notify all parties of what must be done to bring the condition of the title into compliance with the negotiated terms of the sales agreement.

If a specific defect is not removed, it is then listed as an exception on the title insurance coverage policy.

    These defect exceptions are often termed as a cloud on the title or a blemish.

To correct defects of title, some common practices may be used.

Quiet Title Suite	At times, a quite title suit may be undertaken. A quiet title suit is a court ordered hearing to determine land ownership.
Certificate of Title	An attorney may issue a certificate of title that states the opinion of the attorney as to who rightfully owns a parcel of land.
Statute of Frauds	The defect may fall under the Statute of Frauds, which is when the state law requires certain types of contracts to be in writing to be enforceable by law. If the defect is not in writing, it may be cleared through this statute.

Upon the clearing of all defects or clouds, a marketable title is obtained.

If some of the defects that exist within the title cannot be cleared then the defect will be listed as an exception within the title commitment and insurance policy.

The title insurance policy will be created. This creation will be based upon the items that you researched and verified during the completion of your abstractor summary.

The underwriter needs to determine through your research if the title covers the government patent granting the land to the original individual owner. In other words, the underwriter will review your summary documents to confirm that the chain of title is complete.

The underwriter will make a determination based upon your report as to whether the certificate will disclaim the search of any specific records or matters. The wording of the inclusion or disclaimer will be incorporated into the report.

The underwriter will confirm whether the certificate will cover specific times or contains exceptions to any specific times based on all of the data you have remitted.

The legal description of the property will be incorporated into the policy.

This legal description will be the same as the one in the tax rolls.

The description will be drafted directly from the abstracting summary you have completed. It is critical that you copy the description exactly as it appears and confirm that the description you remit is correct.

You must fully understand the nature and extent of legal descriptions. Some descriptions will refer to location and dimension while others may refer to area contents – acreage or square footage.

These are two very distinct variations. Acreage and square footage insurance is very risky in that acreage or square footage is subject to actual boundary questions.

Most title insurance companies are unwilling to issue insurance when the description contains only acreage or square footage descriptions.

The exception to this rule is instances where the amount of money to be paid for the property is contingent on the number of acres or the square footage contained in the property to be insured.

You will be required to obtain and include the legal description for all title commitment and policy paperwork.

An individual qualified under state law will certify the abstract that you completed.

The title commitment will be dated with the same date and time that you noted as the completion date and time for your abstracting summery

This date and time should coincide with the recording of the last instrument that is referred to by the title policy or that creates an interest by the insured.

Any item occurring after you completed your abstracting activity may impede the ability to protect the property.

In other words, if an event occurred after you completed your research you would not have included this event in your abstract report. This makes it impossible for the title underwriter to address the issues that may have occurred, as they have no knowledge of the issue.

The date and time refers to year, month, day, hours, minutes, and seconds.

PROCESSES AND STEPS OF ISSUANCE

- An interested party makes a request or application for an abstract or insurance.

- An examination of public records, registries, indexes, and books to obtain the required information regarding the chain of title of the land to be insured is completed.

- A title commitment is issued based on the result of the abstract or exam of the title.

- The closing or escrow instructions will be reviewed.

- The ability to insure specific risk will be determined using statutory provisions and the underwriting guidelines of specific insurers.

- Exceptions will be eliminated from the policy based upon:

  ➤ Documentation provided

  ➤ Recordation of applicable instruments

  ➤ Statutory provisions

  ➤ Insurance indemnities

- The instruments to be recorded will be reviewed and approved.

- The title insurance policy and any endorsements will be issued.

- The policy premium and other charges are paid.

- The real estate instruments applicable to the transaction will be recorded.

ISSUANCE SPECIFICS

The issuance of a title insurance policy will be based on fact. This issuance must be based on

- The complete search and exam of public records

- The issuance of a valid title commitment

- Insurance of a bona fide purchaser

- Disclosure of all matters that affect the property including knowledge of liens, encumbrances, descent and easements

POLICY COMPONENTS

There are various components to the title binder or title policy. The following listing is a general overview of the title policy contents. Specific forms, policy issues, and statutes may cause alterations to the contents of a particular policy.

COMMITMENTS

Title commitment, commitment, or title binder refers to the binding document issued by the title company that provides formal contract to insure the title. The commitment will contain provisions, conditions, stipulations, and exceptions.

A title commitment may contain various elements depending on the jurisdictional variance where the commitment was issued. The following components are the most common components of a title binder:

The cover showing: Form of policy

Type of policy

Name of the company issuing the policy

The statement of the commitment

The insuring provisions or the basic risks the policy will insure against

General exclusions from the coverage

Conditions of coverage

Stipulations required for coverage

Signatures of officers

Schedule A showing: the commitment number

The effective date of the commitment including the year, month, day, hour, and minute of the commitment

Form and type of policy

Official file number of the policy

The policies the commitment covers

The amount of insurance proposed

Insured estate or interest to be insured

Present ownership
Legal description of the land or estate to be insured

Matters affecting the land that is specifically excepted from the legal description

Notice that policy is only effective if Schedule B is attached

Schedule B showing: Form and type of policy

Policy number

The requirements necessary to create interest

General or standard exceptions

Special exceptions

Authorized signature

AFFIDAVITS

The affidavit is the written declaration of a statement of fact that is made voluntarily and sworn to or affirmed before some person legally authorized to administer an oath or affirmation.

Statutory law establishes the regulations regarding affidavits. These include:

The people who may make affidavits

The authorized individuals who may take affidavits

The requisites for validity of affidavits

The causes that may make an affidavit void

The alternatives to the use of affidavits

In title insurance, affidavits are required and used for a variety of purposes. In general, they are used to

Comply with all statutory provisions

Conform to judicial requirements

Explain defects or omissions of real estate instruments

Supplement the contents of a recorded instrument

Make new information part of the public record

The title insurance underwriter will furnish affidavits to issue the title policy or grant special coverage.

When an affidavit is requested for the insurance of a property, it is important to consider:

Whether the executor (person making the affidavit) is reliable

Whether there is a special form of affidavit required by statute or by the title insurance company specifically.

Whether the information contained in the affidavit will grant special coverage or render a title exception unnecessary.

An affidavit is not a title indemnity.

It is to be used only for explaining or clarifying an issue.

An affidavit may not change or modify a recorded document.

AMOUNT OF THE POLICY

In general, the rules in relation to the permissible amount of a title insurance policy are basic.

The owner's policy may cover the full amount of the purchase price of a property.

There are exceptions to the general rule in that in some cases the owner's policy may not be exact.

Exceptions: If the expected amount of the policy cannot be ascertained at the time, the policy is issued or there are special amount allocations or different non-contiguous tracts are to be insured.

The loan policy may cover the original amount of the mortgage.

The lender policy may vary if the interest over the term of the mortgage is pre-computed and added immediately to the principal amount of the mortgage.

An exception may also occur if the collateral includes personal property, other real property or both, which is not being insured or is being insured.

The policy amount of coverage may also vary depending on whether the policy is being written for the full amount of the mortgage or the policy is being written for an amount less than the amount of the mortgage.

A leasehold policy may be issued.

These policies are subject to criteria set by specific issuing companies.

When a leasehold policy is required, the issuing agent will refer the request to the applicable title insurance underwriter for a determination.

There may be other occurrences where the amount of the title insurance policy is written for a different amount than those listed above. These exceptions occur more rarely and are determined by the particular company or state with which you work.

RELEASE

Many of the specific situations of research that showed a defect in existence or provided a question as to the clarity of the title require the execution of a release.

A release is the relinquishment or giving up of a right, claim or privilege by the person holding the right, claim, or privilege. The term and use of releases vary among jurisdictions. To be valid a release must meet certain requirements. The most common requirements of a valid release are

The use of the correct form as applied by statutory law

Compliance with statutory law concerning wording and contents

Confirmation that the proper individuals executed the release

A thorough description of the claim, privileges, or interests being released

Description of the real property involved in the release if any real property is involved

Recording of the release in the county of record

EXCEPTION

In the case of an exception to the general rule, the specific instance may be noted on Schedule B of the title insurance policy.

The underwriter will provide the proper wording for the exception inclusions.

The wording will be based upon the information you provide so it is vital to the process that your abstract report includes very specific and detailed information regarding all items uncovered during your search process.

ACKNOWLEDGEMENTS

An acknowledgement is the formal statement made before a notary public or other authorized official by anyone who has executed an instrument or document is doing so of his/her own free will. The acknowledgement further shows that the person performing the execution is who they claim to be.

A certificate of acknowledgement is a written statement issued by the notary public or authorized official that the maker of the instrument or document appeared personally before him/her and affirmed the execution as an act of free will and voluntary action.

The certificate of acknowledgement may be printed directly on the instrument being acknowledged or may be a separate document attached to the instrument.

FOREIGN ACKNOWLEDGEMENT

A foreign acknowledgement is an acknowledgement that was taken outside of the state where the land in question is located. This type of acknowledgement is valid as long as it conforms to the laws of the state where the acknowledgement was taken. The laws of the state where the land is located must also authorize the acceptance. This type of acknowledgement may only be recognized in some jurisdictions if a certificate of authenticity or conformity to law issued by the clerk of courts in the county that the acknowledgement was taken.

VALIDITY OF ACKNOWLEDGEMENT

A certificate of acknowledgement and the valid forms of acknowledgement are determined on a state level. The laws of the state in which the acknowledgement is being taken prescribe the requirements.

The general essential elements include

Location where the acknowledgement was taken

Date of the acknowledgement

Name and title of the person taking the acknowledgement

Statement by the notary public or authorized officer that the person making the acknowledgement appeared before him/her personally

Statement that the person making the acknowledgement executed the document of his or her own free will

Marital status of the generator of the acknowledgement

Signature and seal of the notary public or other official

Date the commission of the notary public or other official expires

Any duly qualified notary public or other authorized official may take an acknowledgement

Acknowledgements taken without authority or by parties with an interest in the property are invalid.

Defective acknowledgements must be addressed and cured.

This can be accomplished by the re-acknowledgment and re-filing of the defective instrument by a qualified official or by waiting for the statute of limitations or state marketability act to expire prior to attempting to use that instrument.

It is important to have a thorough knowledge of the processes of acknowledgement because as a rule, an acknowledgement that is defective, whether recorded or not, will not impart actual notice. You must remember however, that even when defective, the acknowledgement cannot be ignored.

If a defective acknowledgement exists, it is important to review the local statutes to determine what requirements exist and if any forms are available for completion concerning the defect.

You should make copies of any statutory or valid forms of acknowledgement and develop an acknowledgements file.

You should also determine the effect of the lack of acknowledgement or defective acknowledgement will have on your subject research property.

ENDORSEMENTS

An endorsement to the title is a written statement issued concerning a title insurance policy or commitment. An endorsement is used to modify the contents and coverage of a title insurance policy. These modifications may include additions, reductions, or deletions to the coverage.

OWNER'S POLICY
SCHEDULE B

Owners Policy Number: OP No: Reference No:

Lender's Policy No: LP No.

This Policy does not insure against loss or damage (and the Company will not pay costs, attorneys' fees or expenses) which arise by reason of the following:

Special Exceptions: The mortgage, if any, referred to in Item 4 of Schedule , and the following exceptions:

1.   Rights or claims of parties in possession not shown by the public records.

2.   Easements, or claims of easements, not shown by the public records.

3.   Any lien, or right to a lien, for services, labor, or materials heretofore or hereafter furnished, imposed by law and not shown by public records.

4.   Encroachments, overlaps, boundary line disputes, or other matters which would be disclosed by an accurate survey or inspection of the premises.

5.   Possible additional assessments for taxes for new construction or for any major improvements pursuant to provisions of Acts of Assembly relating thereto, not yet due and payable.

6.   Subject to all matters, notes, conditions, restrictions, easements, setback and building lines shown on map 0200-19-7B recorded in the Recorder of Deeds Office for THIS County.

7.   Subject to public and private rights in and to all roads and alleys, public or private, if any affecting the subject property.

THIS IS THE END OF SCHEDULE B

Figure 9:7 Sample Form – Title Insurance Schedule B

TITLE INSURANCE VS. TRADITIONAL INSURANCE

Unlike most insurance policies that insure against a future event, title insurance insures against events occurring in the past that may affect the rights of the owner of real property in the future.

Title insurance is a contract of indemnity rather than actual insurance. The title insurance policy is in place to provide defense against litigation affecting the title that is insured and to indemnify any loss experienced by the insured.

To obtain a title insurance policy a one-time premium is paid. This premium covers the entire term of the policy and requires no further payment on the part of the insured.

Title insurance coverage remains in effect until the insured no longer has possession or interest in the title and property being insured.

Title insurance policies may not be assigned or transferred.

The title insurance provides liability coverage only to the individual being insured by the policy.

The title policy only insures against loss or damage resulting from defects in existence prior to the date and time of the policy issuance and not specifically or generally excepted from coverage within the wording of the policy and Schedules.

AFFIRMATIVE INSURANCE

Affirmative insurance may also be known as affirmative coverage and may be referred to as insuring over. This means that coverage is extended to include some defect, lien, encumbrance, or interest that affects the title to the property.

Affirmative insurance is completed by the issuance of appropriate endorsements or by notations at the end of the exceptions.

When affirmative insurance is issued, the outstanding defect, lien encumbrance or interest that affects the title is now insured over.

The language and wording of affirmative insurance must avoid insuring against any consequential damage that might occur on the part of the insured during the existence of the defect, lien, and encumbrance or interest even though the defect, lien, encumbrance, or interest has been removed.

The title insurance underwriter will provide the affirmative authority and language applicable to the affirmative insurance.

The term affirmative insurance is often incorrectly used as a synonym for extended coverage.

Extended coverage refers only to the act of extending the basic coverage of a title insurance policy by not showing or deleting from the policy any exceptions or any exclusion. Extended coverage may also refer to the modification of the provisions of the policy.

When issuing Affirmative Coverage the specific defect, interest, lien, or encumbrance will be specifically excepted in Schedule B of the title policy. The insuring over may also be accomplished through the implementation of an endorsement.

GAP INSURANCE

There is occasionally a time lapse between the date and time of the title commitment and the date and time of the recording of the instruments transferring title. This gap might be a few minutes, hours, or even days. Title insurance policies are typically dated and timed when the recording instruments are issued. Occasionally this is not the case.

When a gap occurs, the title insurance company may issue insurance that provides coverage from the closing of the transaction until the recording of the documents. This is known as gap insurance.

This type of insurance is risky for the insurance company since it is unknown what might occur during the time between the closing of the transaction and the recording of the instrument.

This insurance is provided through an endorsement to the title and the underwriter on the file will determine the wording and issuance.

COINSURANCE

Two different forms of co-insurance may be issued on a particular file.

1.   The first policy divides the risk between the insurer and the insured. This form of insurance represents a divided risk between the title insurance company and the insured. The insurance company insures a percentage of the risk while the insurer insures the remainder in a self-insured manner.

2.   The second type of co-insurance is insurance where two or more insurance companies divide the risk of insurance between them. This method requires that two or more insurance companies insure the same insured concerning the same interest in land. Both companies will provide identical coverage.

EXTENDED COVERAGE

In title insurance, extended coverage refers to the deletion or removal of any or all of the general or specific exceptions contained in Schedule B of the title commitment.

BELATED COVERAGE

At times, an owner already in possession of the property will request insurance of the title. This event brings to note additional items that must be considered.

In case of insurance for an owner already in possession of the property, the insured would not be considered a bona fide purchaser.

The request for insurance at this late time is also suspect. It may be considered that the insurance request is a result of the owner learning about a title defect, lien or encumbrance not previously brought to light or that an outsider is claiming a right to the title.

To insure an owner already in possession some additional factors should be ascertained:

Why is the owner seeking coverage now?

Are parties other than those of record occupying the property or a portion of the property?

Does the examination of the title bring to light any previously undiscovered liens, encumbrances, pending suits or other matters affecting the title?

Was there a previous title insurance policy procured against the property or mortgage to the property?

In addition to these items of research, the owner in possession should execute an affidavit of title and adverse possession.

This affidavit should state that the owner seeking coverage has no knowledge of any claim, lien, encumbrance, or other matter affecting the property except those shown in public record or specifically excepted with in the commitment and policy.

Other specifics to providing coverage to the owner in possession may exist. You should consult with the title underwriter to determine additional search and exception actions that may be required.

CHAPTER

10

UNDERSTANDING YOUR PERSONALITY

At the beginning of this course, we highlighted specific characteristics title companies will look for in a title abstractor. Your personality plays an essential role in determining what specific characteristics will apply to you in personal, career and higher stress situations.

The following pages will assist you in better understanding the inherent characteristics that apply to your specific personality type and sub-type. We encourage you to capitalize on the strengths inherent in your personality type and to understand the potential roadblocks specific characteristics may create in your pathway to career success.

There are no true personality weaknesses in the information you are about to review. There is, however, incredible opportunity for understanding yourself, gaining the ability to create the environment that will assist you on the path to success, and modifying your behavior to minimize potential roadblocks on the path to success. The profiles will also assist you in learning how best to handle the diversity you will encounter in individuals you work with on a daily basis.

Each of us has heard people make reference to a Type A personality. We say someone is a Dynamic Person or an Innovative Individual. Some of you may have been in situations where you are categorized as one type of personality or another.

Do you know what the personality classifications mean?

Have you learned the characteristics that often relate to these personality classifications?

Do you know which category characterizes your personality?

Do you understand the benefits that can be gained by altering your environment and outside influences to bring forth certain aspects of your personality in specific situations and minimizing other, less effective characteristics?

We are going to review the various terms for personality typing popularized through the years and the characteristics that define these terms. This section will provide you with valuable insight into the motivations, strengths, and general characteristics of each main personality type that you may encounter during the day.

You should be able to determine the influence each personality type will have on your ability to succeed. You will also learn what personality designation characterizes your primary and secondary typing and the actions you can take to assist you in using the benefits of your personality typing to assist you on the path to success.

An important point that you should understand is that there are no wrong or right personalities.

Each type of personality carries with it various strengths as well as obstacles.

Years of research have provided tools that you can use to turn these obstacles into strengths.

Another point to keep in mind is that no person can be characterized as totally one personality type or another. We each have a primary classification and secondary classifications. Some of us even have a different classification under stress than we do when we feel relaxed. Today we will review only the primary classifications.

Each of the primary classifications can also be considered secondary classifications. Once you have completed the worksheets and designated your primary classification you can easily designate your secondary classification by calculating the second highest figure on your answer sheet. If you carry the course one-step further by reviewing how your primary and secondary classifications interact with each other, you can gain additional insight into your actions, motivational triggers, and even stress-related obstacles. Additional, advanced training is available that will assist you in identifying, honing and minimizing various aspects of your personality.

The first step in the process is to complete the question sheet that you will find on the following pages. You will be the only person who reviews the results so please, be honest with yourself. You will learn valuable information that will assist you in obtaining your goals and become better skilled at analysis of others leading to greater interpersonal success.

To complete the test, review each question and the descriptive words supplied.

Consider your behavior and actions as they relate to the work environment.

Circle the one word out of each group that best describes your actions during work related activities.

You can locate the personality codes on the answer key following the test. These codes will correlate to the basic analysis charts included in this Chapter.

1. When I arrive for work I feel: Eager Bold Introspective Content	2. I work best when I am given: Defined Goals Recognition Authority Routine
3. I want my supervisor to provide: Direct Answers Sincere Appreciation Freedom of Expression Specific Recognition	4. Sometimes I focus too much on: Details Influencing Others Obtaining Results Cooperation
5. My career must provide: Challenge Accuracy Interaction Stability	6. I approach each task with: Consistency Problem Solving Critical Analysis Motivation
7. Co-workers describe me as: Inspiring Amiable Stable Competitive	8. When faced with an unusual idea I feel: Receptive Impulsive Detailed Adventurous
9. My greatest strength is: Persistence Expression Self-Reliance Competence	10. My team sees me as: Decisive Diplomatic Cooperative Group Oriented
11. As a team leader my style is: Inspirational Patient Logical Results Oriented	12. To motivate others I employ: Conscientiousness Persuasiveness Consideration Directness
13. When I arrive at work I feel: Eager Independent Self-Reliant Loyal	14. I work best with: Predictable routines Clear expectations Challenge Freedom
15. Under pressure I sometimes become: Outspoken Precise Detailed Inspiring	16. My conversational style is: Chatty Amiable Rational Direct

Figure 10:1 Sample Form – Personality Profile Testing Page 1

17. When receiving a compliment I feel:		18. I am pleased when others say I am:	
Modest	Uneasy	Accomplished	Charming
Poised	Non-Committal	Logical	Loyal
19. I enjoy the role of:		20. When completing a difficult task I become:	
Entertainer	Leader	Concise	Determined
Listener	Diplomat	Persuasive	Amiable
21. I focus on:		22. I react to the problems of others with:	
Accuracy	Results	Emotion	Sympathy
People	Consistency	Decisiveness	Sensitivity
23. I sometimes forget to:		24. At business functions I am:	
Pace Myself	Request Recognition	Amiable	Social
Use Time Management	Think outside the box	Reserved	Intense
25. I am inspired by:		26. I may be too concerned with:	
Popularity	Peace	Status	Control
Perfection	Power	Comfort	Ability
27. I perform best when I am:		28. Sometimes I think I am too:	
Order Setting	Analyzing	Serious	Sensitive
Socializing	Perceiving	Insensitive	Excitable
29. I enjoy being described as:		30. When waiting to begin a new task I feel:	
Self-Confident	Aggressive	Impatient	Anxious
Relaxed	Conscientious	Exuberant	Humble

Figure 10:2 Sample Form – Personality Profile Testing Page 2

Assess your answers against the following key. The letter that corresponds to your testing answers most frequently will be considered your primary personality characteristic. Once you feel comfortable with the understanding of your primary personality typing you may assess your secondary personality by calculating the second highest scoring letter on your testing key.

1. When I arrive for work I feel:		2. I work best when I am given:	
Eager S	Determined C	Defined Goals M	Recognition S
Introspective M	Content P	Authority C	Routine P

3. I want my supervisor to provide:		4. Sometimes I focus too much on:	
Direct Answers C	Sincere Appreciation P	Details M	Influencing Others S
Freedom of Expression S	Specific Recognition M	Obtaining Results C	Cooperation P

5. My career must provide:		6. I approach each task with:	
Challenge C	Accuracy M	Consistency P	Problem Solving C
Interaction S	Stability P	Critical Analysis M	Motivation S

7. Co-workers describe me as:		8. When faced with an unusual idea I feel:	
Inspiring S	Amiable P	Receptive P	Impulsive S
Stable M	Competitive C	Detailed M	Adventurous C

9. My greatest strength is:		10. My team sees me as:	
Persistence M	Expression S	Decisive C	Diplomatic M
Self-Reliance C	Competence C	Cooperative P	Group Oriented S

11. As a team leader my style is:		12. To motivate others I employ:	
Inspirational S	Patient P	Conscientiousness M	Persuasiveness S
Logical M	Results Oriented C	Consideration P	Directness C

13. When I arrive at work I feel:		14. I work best with:	
Eager S	Independent M	Predictable Routines S	Clear Expectations C
Self-Reliant C	Loyal P	Challenge D	Freedom I

15. Under pressure I sometimes become:		16. My conversational style is:	
Outspoken C	Precise P	Chatty S	Amiable P
Detailed M	Inspiring S	Rational M	Direct C

Figure 10:3 Sample Form – Personality Profile Answer Key Page 1

17. When receiving a compliment I feel:		18. I am pleased when others say I am:	
Modest P	Uneasy C	Accomplished C	Charming S
Poised S	Non-Committal M	Logical M	Loyal P
19. I enjoy the role of:		**20. When completing a difficult task I become:**	
Entertainer S	Leader C	Concise M	Determined C
Listener P	Diplomat M	Persuasive S	Amiable P
21. I focus on:		**22. I react to the problems of others with:**	
Accuracy P	Results C	Emotion S	Sympathy P
People S	Consistency M	Decisiveness C	Sensitivity M
23. I sometimes forget to:		**24. At business functions I am:**	
Pace Myself C	Request Recognition P	Amiable M	Social S
Use Time Management S	Think outside the box M	Reserved P	Intense C
25. I am inspired by:		**26. I may be too concerned with:**	
Popularity S	Peace P	Status S	Control C
Perfection M	Power C	Comfort P	Ability M
27. I perform best when I am:		**28. Sometimes I think I am too:**	
Order Setting C	Analyzing M	Serious M	Sensitive P
Socializing S	Perceiving P	Insensitive C	Excitable S
29. I enjoy being described as:		**30. When waiting to begin a new task I feel:**	
Self-Confident S	Aggressive C	Impatient C	Anxious P
Relaxed P	Conscientious M	Exuberant S	Humble M

Figure 10:4 Sample Form – Personality Profile Answer Key Page 2

POPULAR TERMS IDENTIFYING PERSONALITY

Common Terms: Answer C	Common Terms: Answer S
Dominant Choleric Type A	Dynamic Sanguine Expresser
Descriptive Words:	**Descriptive Words:**
Direct	Influential
Self-propelled	Dynamic
Driver	Expressive
Accomplishment	Impulsive
Accuracy	Emotional
Forceful	Generous
Risk Taker	Poised
Self-reliant	Persuasive
Leadership	Captivating
Adventurous	Enthusiastic
Decisive	Friendly
Competitive	Inspiring
Common Terms: Answer P	**Common Terms: Answer M**
Solid Phlegmatic Idealist	Analytical Melancholy Systematic
Descriptive Words:	**Descriptive Words:**
Competent	Steadiness
Innovative	Analytical
Amiable	Rational
Receptive	Perfectionist
Steadiness	Diplomatic
Traditional	Sensitive
Modest	Mature
Considerate	Independent
Loyal	Persistent
Patient	Conscientious
Sympathetic	Precise
Neighborly	Thorough

As you can see from the descriptive words used for each personality type, each has its own strengths. Each personality type provides specific benefits within the workplace.

A keen understanding of the situations in which your personality type works the best is the next step toward implementing your career building skills. You will want to foster a work environment that generates the highest level of successful activity for your personality type.

A secondary consideration is that you should attempt to surround yourself with individuals whose personality characteristics naturally stimulate you to perform to your optimal peak expectations. The following pages will assist you in determining the best working environment for you and the individuals whose inherent characteristics can assist you on the pathway to success.

DOMINANT/CHOLERIC/TYPE A PERSONALITY

A dominant or choleric personality type is often referred to as a Type A personality. We hear this term and even use this term in relationship to certain individuals. This personality is typically the easiest to identify.

These individuals will bring exceptional focus and a drive for results to the workplace.

A choleric or Type A personality will focus on obtaining results. At times, the choleric person will focus so strongly on obtaining results that they will fail to pay strict attention to the feelings and ideas of others.

To obtain the best results a choleric personality must obtain:

> Direct answers to their questions
> Freedom to perform to their best without constraints or controls
> The power and authority to implement their ideas
> A variety of tasks, which contain diverse activities
> The ability to gain prestige and advancement for their activities
> Challenge

When properly focused the choleric personality will provide:

> Immediate results
> Exceptional problem solving skills and group leadership
> Quick decisions
> Focused action and project attention

When you determine that you are a choleric personality, you will need to pair yourself with individuals who can provide a balance to the strong drive inherent to the Type A personality. This will assist you in functioning at your most effective level. Partners and groups working with a choleric should include individuals whom:

> Use caution.
> Promote structure.
> Use practical experience.
> Pace themselves and others

DYNAMIC/SANGUIN/EXPRESSOR PERSONALITY

A dynamic or sanguine personality type is often referred to as an expresser or performer personality. We hear this term and even use this term in relationship to certain individuals. This personality is typically the center of a group.

These individuals will perform vital functions to put others at ease with the goal of influencing or persuading others to view projects, tasks, and activities from their prospective.

A dynamic or sanguine personality will focus on motivating and influencing people. The sanguine person occasionally focuses so strongly on the social interactions and the impression others have of them that they will loose track of time.

To obtain the best results a sanguine personality must obtain:

> Recognition and positive reinforcement
> Social situations and group projects
> Freedom to express themselves

When properly focused the sanguine personality will provide:

> Enthusiasm
> Motivation and positive attitudes in team projects or group situations
> Group participation
> Democratic policies that include mentoring and coaching

A sanguine personality you will function at their best when paired with individuals who can provide a balance to the focus on appearance and personality in the dynamic personality. Partners and groups working with a sanguine should include individuals whom:

> Implement time management technique
> Prioritizes tasks
> Use logic and planning for task management
> Speak directly.

SOLID/PHLEGMATIC/IDEALIST PERSONALITY

A phlegmatic or idealist personality type is often referred to as a solid or amiable personality. This personality is typically the most cooperative individual and will expend great focus on the execution of each task.

These individuals will bring team building skills, task management follow-through and a solid dependable routine to the workplace.

A solid or phlegmatic personality will focus on the methodical completion of a task and group cooperation. At times, the idealist person will focus so strongly on the details of a particular task; they will need validation of the worth of their efforts. The solid personality often requires discussion concerning how their efforts contribute to the project as a whole.

To obtain the best results a solid personality must obtain:

Sincere appreciation for your efforts
Standard routines and clearly outlined procedures.
Guidelines for accomplishing tasks and encouragement of creative endeavors

When properly focused the idealist personality will provide:

Consistent work output
Stability and a calming influence in group situations
A sincere desire to assist others
Minimal conflict and intense identification with a group

As an idealist personality, you function at your best when paired with individuals who are of a similar level of competence. The partners of an individual with an idealist personality must have the ability to assist in prioritizing tasks and moving projects toward completion. Partners and groups working with an idealist should include individuals whom:

Implement time management technique
Prioritizes tasks
Use logic and planning for task management
Promote recognition of the group's accomplishments

ANALYTICAL/MELONCHOLY/SYSTEMATIC PERSONALITY

A melancholy or systematic personality type is often referred to as an analytical or conscientious individual. This personality is typically the most dedicated to ensuring quality and accuracy in the completion of each task. This personality type may be the most naturally suited to the career of title abstractor.

These individuals will bring analytical thinking, diplomacy and an attention to detail to each task and to the office.

To work best this personality type must understand the motivating factors that affect their performance.

A systematic or melancholy personality will focus on the quality and accuracy of each project or task and will work with groups to ensure diplomatic relations are maintained. At times, the systematic person will focus so strongly on the details of a task that they will lose focus of the overall project.

To obtain the best results a choleric personality must obtain:

> Clearly defined goals and expectations
> A reserved and professional atmosphere with minimal conflict
> Recognition for specific skills and accomplishments

When properly focused the idealist personality will provide:

> Diplomacy and a cooperative attitude with a group
> Focused attention to details and standards
> Critical analysis of personal and group performance
> Respect for the worth of individuals as well as their accomplishments.

As a systematic personality, you will function at your best when paired or working with individuals who are able to make decisions quickly. The partners of an individual with a systematic personality must have the ability to assist in prioritizing tasks and delegating specific aspects of the task. Partners and groups working with an idealist should include individuals whom:

> Decisively determine direction and focus.
> Look beyond guidelines to promote creative activity.
> Initiate group discussion ensuring all parties maintain involvement in the project
> Encourage team-building attitudes.

APPENDIX A

Real Estate TITLE SEARCH - Abstracting Workbook

Abstracting Overview - Review Questions

1. A title search must have the ability to:

2. Advanced abstracting duties might include:

3. Give the three characteristics most frequently sought in a title abstractor:

4. Give the three most common career choices for a newly trained title abstractor:

5. The primary concern of a title abstractor is:

6. Your abstract of title will include activities that affect the title from:

7.   The primary duty of a title abstractor is:

_____
_____
_____
_____
_____
_____

8.   What two specific determinations will be made based upon your abstracting report?

_____
_____
_____
_____
_____
_____

9.   _____ and _____ base their entire process around the work that you perform during your research

10.   The career of real estate title abstractor is _____ to the _____ of the real estate title insurance and closing industries and as such requires _____, _____, and _____ practices on your part.

11.   A competent title researcher must be able to
       a.   document the status of any defects
       b.   review and establish a chain of title
       c.   carefully and accurately search public records
       d.   all of the above

12.   Advanced abstracting duties might include
       a.   the issuance of title policies
       b.   the creation of title commitments
       c.   the underwriting of specific issues to a property
       d.   all of the above

13.   An abstractor does not need to
       a.   provide dedication to the concise completion of each task
       b.   provide a methodical approach to task completion
       c.   customize their business process around their lifestyle
       d.   bring high levels of focus to their workflow

14.   Positions in the title industry are
       a.   rewarding
       b.   secure
       c.   flexible
       d.   all of the above

15.   Gaining an understanding of the overall task is more important than an attention to detail.
       a.   True
       b.   False

Real Property Review Questions

1.   What are the three rights that may be transferred or severed from the transfer of land?

_____
_____
_____
_____
_____
_____

2.   Name the four standards to be applied when determining if an item is considered a fixture:

_____
_____
_____
_____
_____
_____

3.   Explain a reason that a fixture might not be insurable as part of the title commitment even when the real property contains no liens:

_____
_____
_____
_____
_____
_____

4.   The term severance when applied to real property rights and interests means:

_____
_____
_____
_____
_____
_____

5.   Real property _____ rights include the _____ that exist and area actually _____ to the surface of the land.

6.   A _____ is a piece of personal property that has been _____, _____ OR _____ _____ to a parcel of land or the structures on the land.

7.   Crops are also known as _____ or _____

8.   A property's _____ is effected its ability to transfer _____ to the new purchaser.

9.   Sub-surface resources are subject to the same rights of _____ as any _____ portion of the land.

10.   If an item is classified as _____ _____, it will not be included in the sale of real property.

11.   The severance of a resource right may be completed by
        a.   Conveyance or grant
        b.   A lease of the named rights
        c.   Adverse possession
        d.   All of the above

12. Sub-surface rights typically include the right to all of the following except:
    a.   The right to sell crops
    b.   The right to enter beneath the surface of the land
    c.   The right to lease mineral rights to another
    d.   All of the above

13. Which item is typically not included with air rights?
    a.   Electrical Wires
    b.   Roofs
    c.   Tree Limbs
    d.   Air above the property

14. Possible transfers of airspace would include the sale of
    a.   Navigational easements
    b.   Mineral Rights
    c.   Water rights
    d.   Both A and C

15. Which of the following does not describe land rights?
    a.   It is possible for one person to own the air rights and subsurface rights only
    b.   A person can own the surface rights exclusively
    c.   Only a company or the government can own mineral rights
    d.   A person can own air, surface and sub-surface rights independently

16. Surface rights are commonly referred to as:
    a.   The right to the land and the improvements of the land
    b.   The right to what is beneath the land
    c.   The right to what is above the land
    d.   All of the above

17. Improvements may include:
    a.   Pipelines
    b.   Pavement
    c.   Buildings
    d.   All of the above

18. Which of the following is not considered real property?
    a.   A dresser
    b.   Trees
    c.   A fence
    d.   None of the above

19. What standard is not applied when determining if an item is a fixture?
    a.   The interpretation of a real estate agent
    b.   The intention of the parties who own the property
    c.   The manner in which the item is attached to the real property
    d.   An agreement between the parties in the transaction

20. What is not typically a reason an owner might sever a specific right from the bundle of rights?
    a.   To build additional structures
    b.   To reduce taxes
    c.   To create a leaseback transaction
    d.   To increase the value of a property

Hennin

Land and Descriptions Review Questions

1. Name the methods of land descriptions you will encounter during the title search process.

2. The method that provides land description through street numbers and place names is known as INFORMAL REFERENCE and the primary advantage of this method of description is:

3. Direction is shown as:

4. The point where a parcel survey begins is frequently termed the:

5. The RECTANGULAR SUVEY SYSTEM is also termed:

6. What method of surveying is used to describe the most landmass in the United States?

7. A check or quadrangle contains how many miles?

8. Define a survey:

    _____
    _____
    _____
    _____
    _____

9. Who sets the standards and requirements for surveyors in the United States?

    _____
    _____
    _____
    _____
    _____

10. The _____ method begins at a _____, which is a permanent reference mark.

11. Distance and direction is another term for _____ ___ _____
    _____.

12. It is customary to describe a parcel by going _____.

13. Latitude lines run _____-_____ while longitude lines run _____-_____.

14. Another term for the lot-block-tract system is the _____.
    _____.

15. The _____ _____ _____ is a number assigned by the tax assessor to aid in tax collection.

16. An informal reference is
    a. Numbers and names of streets used to describe a property
    b. A monument set at one corner of a parcel
    c. Degrees, minutes and seconds
    d. All of the above

17. How many people will typically conduct a survey?
    a. 1
    b. 3
    c. 2
    d. All of the above

18. A rectangular survey uses
    a. Degrees
    b. Principal Meridians
    c. Lot-Block Tracts
    d. All of the above

19. Which survey method uses a unit of measurement termed checks?
    a. Rectangular survey
    b. Metes and Bounds survey
    c. Recorded Plat survey
    d. All of the above

20.   What method is most frequently used to define a parcel?
     a.   Rectangular Survey
     b.   Metes and Bounds
     c.   Recorded Plat
     d.   None of the above

21.   Which of the following includes the current owner's name, address and the assessed value of the improvements to the property?
     a.   Recorded Plat
     b.   Assessor's Parcel
     c.   Metes and Bounds
     d.   All of the above

22.   A survey drawing does not show
     a.   Improvements
     b.   Easements
     c.   Features
     d.   Mortgages

23.   What survey method uses degrees, minutes and seconds?
     a.   Rectangular survey
     b.   Recorded plat
     c.   Metes and Bounds
     d.   None of the above

24.   An acre contains how many square feet?
     a.   49,650
     b.   33,650
     c.   43,650
     d.   39,650

25.   A square mile contains how many square acres?
     a.   640
     b.   650
     c.   540
     d.   All of the above

Access and Rights Review Questions

1.   All access points relating to the property being researched should:

2.   Physical access is:

3.   Legal access is:

4.   When you begin your research activity with regard to access it is best to:

5.   Define accretion

6.   List the three items you must specifically research in relationship to beach property.

7.   A riparian right is a right that occurs when a property borders a _____ or _____.

8.   A littoral right is a right that occurs when a property borders a _____ OR _____.

9.   The _____ of _____ _____ may come into effect that allows the first landowner that diverts water for his use to continue this diversion although it is not fair to other landowners.

10. A common _____ would be an _____ or right-of-way that was gained for that particular parcel of land.

11. What term describes the situation where a property touches another piece of real estate or a public road?
    a. Legal access
    b. Physical access
    c. Abut
    d. All of the above

12. The most common situations that create boundary line issues include
    a. Improper location of fences
    b. Accreted land
    c. Defective legal descriptions
    d. All of the above

13. An additional right that may be granted to a property bordering water is
    a. Riparian right
    b. Accretion Right
    c. Egress
    d. All of the above

14. The alteration to a waterway for individual use may be allowed under the doctrine of prior appropriation
    a. True
    b. False

15. The most common boundary line problems occur due to
    a. Errors in surveys
    b. Riparian rights
    c. Abutters rights
    d. All of the above

16. If a right of way is not visible in any public record, you should consult with the underwriter assigned to the file to determine what additional items of research may be required.
    a. True
    b. False

17. If a property abuts a road, it automatically gains access to that road.
    a. True
    b. False

18. A matter that impairs the right of access to a property must be
    a. covered under easement insurance
    b. noted and specifically excepted in schedule B
    c. linked to an adjoining property
    d. all of the above

19. An abstractor's only concern with regard to access to a property is whether it is accessible by vehicle.
    a. True
    b. False

20. If an issue exists with regard to tax assessment or property description, you must note the proper exception on the errors in survey report.
    a. True
    b. False

Real Estate Title Search - Abstracting

Estates - Review Questions

1.   Name the two parties who obtain rights to property:

2.   Define the term encumbrance.

3.   Explain the use of inheritance tax.

4.   Explain the use of estate tax.

5.   The system of governing estates in the US most closely resembles the _____ _____.

6.   The highest and most complete form of estate ownership is the _____ _____, which is typically transferred using a _____ _____ _____.

7.   A life estate provides a _____ _____ to use and occupy a property and when it ends, the estate reverts to the original grantor who is also known as the _____.

8.   The concept of real estate ownership can be easiest understood when you view ownership as a _____ ____ _____ or collection of rights to ownership.

9.   The abstract report is specifically concerned with rights that are _____ as well as rights that are _____ in a real estate transfer.

10.   If a person dies without a will or having disposed of their property, the laws of intestacy property will come into effect. This is also known as the _____ _____ _____ _____ _____.

11.   Rights may be fully bundled at the time of transfer
    a.   True
    b.   False

12. Ownership in the freehold estate ends at the owner's death
    a.   True
    b.   False

13. What type of estate is contingent on the occurrence of a specific event?
    a.   Life Estate
    b.   Determinable Fee Estate
    c.   Leasehold Estate
    d.   All of the above

14. Title is a synonym for
    a.   Bundle of rights
    b.   Ownership
    c.   Eminent Domain
    d.   None of the above

15. Fee simple estates are not inheritable
    a.   True
    b.   False

16. When another obtains a claim against a persons estate is a (n)
    a.   Escheat
    b.   Encumbrance
    c.   Domain
    d.   None of the above

17. When you locate an encumbrance, you should make a mental note in the event it becomes an issue at a later date
    a.   True
    b.   False

18. If unpaid inheritance taxes exist, you should
    a.   Note the existence on your report
    b.   Request an exception on the title commitment
    c.   Request the taxes be paid according to statute
    d.   Any of the above

19 When researching estates, you should focus on
    a.   the acts of the current owner
    b.   the acts of the previous owners
    c.   the tax payment status
    d.   all of the above

20. If a person dies without a valid will, you should
    a.   Make a note for the underwriter
    b.   Confirm the statutes of descent and distribution were followed
    c.   Review the invalid will and note any issues for the underwriter
    d.   All of the above

Estate Limitations Review Questions

1.   The term bundle of rights refers to:

2.   Name four rights retained by the government.

3.   Explain how a deed restriction or _____may be enforced

4.   Give the explanation for an easement by prescription:

5.   The government right of _____ _____ is imposed to protect the health, _____ and _____ _____of the public.

6.   An example of government _____ ___ _____occurs when the government is acting to control a flood area and runs a drainage pipe _____ or _____ another's property.

7.   The non-payment of _____ _____may result in the government seizure of property resulting in the loss of an owner's interest. This occurs in an attempt to gain the needed revenue for specific operations.

8.   The process of _____ _____ is the taking of a piece of private property for _____ _____.

9.   If an individual loses the ability to enjoy full use of his property through the actions of another, he may bring an _____ _____suit.

10.   An easement grants the right to _____ _____ a certain portion of privately owned property.

11.   A bundle of rights is
        a.   the level of interest one loses to police power
        b.   the level of interest one has in real property
        c.   the interest a property owner has after a sale
        d.   none of the above

12. The bundle of rights cannot be broken.
    a. True
    b. False

13. It is the job of the abstractor to determine what limitations are imposed on the bundle of rights
    a. True
    b. False

14. Limitations in the owner's rights may be imposed by
    a. Public Sources
    b. Private Sources
    c. Both public and private sources
    d. None of the above

15. Government condemnation can be created by
    a. a deed restriction
    b. an easement
    c. a flood zone
    d. all of the above

16. Real estate taxes provide funds for
    a. upcoming elections
    b. special interest projects
    c. public benefits
    d. all of the above

17. An integral part of the abstractor function is verification of the status of the taxes
    a. True
    b. False

18. The abstractor should note the
    a. location and description of an easement
    b. the wording of an easement
    c. the parties granting and gaining an easement
    d. all of the above

19. It is important that the abstractor fully note and describe any limitations discovered while researching the chain of title.
    a. True
    b. False

20. An abstractor does not need to locate the final status of limitations including easements if they have adequately documented the wording and location of the information.
    a. True
    b. False

Forms of Ownership Review Questions

1.   The types of ownership are important for you to understand so that you may:

2.   Name the _____ unities that may exist in this type of ownership.

3.   Name three forms of this type of tenancy.

4.   Name five special entity or individual owners whose interests in real property may require special items of scrutiny on the part of the abstractor.

5.   Sole ownership may be held by

6.   Tenancy by Severalty is also known as _____ _____ and means that the ownership of a property is

7.   Concurrent ownership is ownership held by _____ or more individuals.

8.   The term _____ refers to the administration of the property and interest of a _____ or _____ individual.

9.   A title company may occasionally rely on either an _____ or _____ agreement for the elimination of the marital rights of a spouse.

10. Any action taken by _____ interested owner will affect the title to the _____ you are researching

11. Tenancy by Severalty means there are
    a. Two owners
    b. Many Owners
    c. One Owner
    d. All of the above

12. Concurrent owners share
    a. The property
    b. Unity
    c. Ownership interest
    d. All of the above

13. Tenancy in common occurs
    a. Without the right of survivorship
    b. When ownership is held by two or more individuals
    c. With the unity of possession
    d. All of the above

14. Any owner of a property may
    a. Incur liens
    b. Convey interest
    c. Create a condemnation
    d. All of the above

15. An Ante nuptial agreement
    a. Does not affect property ownership
    b. Does not affect disposition of property
    c. Does not affect the research process
    d. None of the above

16. Any entity transferring property
    a. Must have legal right to hold title to real property
    b. May be empowered by escheat to transfer property
    c. Must advertise the transfer
    d. All of the above

Liens and Encumbrances Review Questions

1.   Name the two types of liens you will encounter during your search and describe them.

_____
_____
_____
_____
_____

2.   Name four types of judgments you may encounter in your search process.

_____
_____
_____
_____
_____
_____

3.   A mortgage lien is created when:

_____
_____
_____
_____
_____
_____
_____

4.   A foreclosure proceeding is

_____
_____
_____
_____
_____
_____

5.   Liens are prioritized by _____ and this order dictates that

_____
_____
_____
_____
_____
_____

6.   A _____ _____ goes against an individual and attaches to all of the _____ _____ of that individual within the county.

7.   A _____ _____ goes against a specific property.

8.   The lien that always comes first in the order of priority regardless of the time is the _____ _____.

9.   If you locate a judgment lien with regard to the property you are searching, you should research to determine if the judgment has been _____.

10.   The _____ _____ law gives anyone that has furnished _____ or _____ for the improvement of a parcel of land the right to place a lien against the improvements and the land.

11. What type of lien is created against a property when an owner uses it as collateral to borrower money?
    a.   General Lien
    b.   Voluntary Lien
    c.   Involuntary Lien
    d.   All of the above

12. A general lien goes against an individual and does not impact real property
    a.   True
    b.   False

13. Which of the following best describes a real estate property tax lien?
    a.   Voluntary Lien
    b.   General Lien
    c.   Specific Lien
    d.   All of the above

14. A property tax lien can be attached to multiple properties.
    a.   True
    b.   False

15. When a property is sold by order of the court it is termed a
    a.   Judgment Lien
    b.   Foreclosure
    c.   Escheat
    d.   All of the above

16. Liens may be imposed against
    a.   Fixtures
    b.   Improvements
    c.   Real Property
    d.   All of the above

7. Which type of sale gives the purchaser a lien against the property for the taxes, assessed fees and interest owing from unpaid real estate tax assessments?
    a.   Foreclosure Sale
    b.   Judicial Sale
    c.   Subject To Sale
    d.   None of the above

18. Tax liens are similar to mechanics liens and voluntary liens in that they are recorded and paid in order of priority.

    a.   True
    b.   False

Deeds Review Questions

1.   Explain the purpose of a deed.

2.   What is considered the best deed a buyer can obtain from a seller?

3.   What does a grant deed warrant?

4.   What does a bargain and sale deed warrant?

5.   What is the purpose of a correction deed?

6.   The physical transfer of a deed before the death of the grantor is known as

7.   List five of the most common covenants you may find in a deed of transfer.

8.   Explain the purpose of an exception in a deed.

9.   The basic _____ and _____ deed contains no covenants and only the minimal essentials of the deed.

10.   Each _____ on the deed and the _____ _____, inclusions and type of deed within the public records of the property you are researching will affect the rights of any future owner of that property.

11.   A general warranty deed is the lowest form of deed.
       a.   True
       b.   False

12.   A quitclaim deed
       a.   contains no warranties
       b.   contains no covenants
       c.   does not promise the seller even holds interest in the property
       d.   all of the above

13.   A cession deed is a form of
       a.   General Warranty Deed
       b.   Quitclaim Deed
       c.   Guardians Deed
       d.   None of the above

14.   Reservations in the deed are made in favor of
       a.   the Government
       b.   the Grantee
       c.   the Grantor
       d.   the Taxing Authority

15.   A deed restriction may limit
       a.   the action of a lender
       b.   the action of the owner
       c.   the action of an investor
       d.   all of the above

16.   The abstractor should review all documents and note any exception, restriction or other matter that may limit the rights of an owner.
       a.   True
       b.   False

Understanding Contracts Review Questions

1.   What does a real estate sales contract outline?

2.   List five common alternate names you might encounter for a real estate sales contract.

3.   List three alternate names commonly used for the contract for deed.

4.   Under a contract for deed who holds legal title to the property?

5.   What does the buyer gain under a contract for deed?

6.   Who may assign their interest in the property under a contract for deed?

7.   Explain the purpose of an option to purchase.

8. What three possible avenues must you explore when you discover an option to purchase in the chain of title?

    _____
    _____
    _____
    _____
    _____

9. Unless an issue arises, deeds are the only legal documents you must review in the title search process.
    a. True
    b. False

10. Equitable title is
    a. a title that is fair and provides an even interest to all parties
    b. an interest created between the recording of the sales agreement and the deed
    c. a synonym for the abstract of title
    d. none of the above

11. The status of all sales contracts should be researched.
    a. True
    b. False

12. You can confirm that a sales contract was terminated by locating
    a. proof of the sale and acquisition by the buyer named
    b. a judicial decree terminating the contract
    c. a recording instrument terminating the contract
    d. any of the above

13. Another name you may locate for a contact for deed is
    a. installment land contract
    b. acquisition contract
    c. purchaser option
    d. any of the above

14. When a contract for deed exists, you should note
    a. the existence of the contract
    b. the parties to the contract
    c. the condition of the contract
    d. all of the above

15. If a contract that has not been terminated exists in record, options may include
    a. obtaining a judicial decree
    b. obtaining a seller declaration of forfeiture
    c. obtaining an executed release from the buyer
    d. any of the above

16. An option may be removed from exception requirements if
    a. the option has expired
    b. the underwriter deems the risk at a low level
    c. the option holder has died
    d. any of the above

Conducting the Search Review Questions

1.   How is constructive notice given?

2.   Actual notice is the knowledge that one has actually gained based on what is:

3.   When completing an abstract of title you will begin with:

4.   What can be found on a tract index page?

5.   How are grantor indexes arranged:

6.   Explain the concept of a chain of title.

7.   What action will you take if you discover a break (missing item) within the chain of title?

8.   Constructive notice is accomplished by the _____ of a document at the county recorder office.

9.   The simplest indexes to use are the_____ _____.

10.   The documents presented for recording will be _____ and the copies will be placed in the _____ with indexes.

       The book and index _____ will be noted on the _____.

11.   Constructive notice is not accomplished by
       a.   Visibly occupying the property
       b.   Recording a document within public record
       c.   Public notice within the mandated advertising media
       d.   All of the above

12.   Inquiry notice is the responsibility of
       a.   The purchaser of a property
       b.   The owner of a property
       c.   The taxing authority
       d.   All of the above

13.   Actual notice is gained by what is
       a.   Observed
       b.   Heard
       c.   Seen
       d.   All of the above

14.   A tract index allocates
       a.   One page to a parcel or land group
       b.   One page to each property owner
       c.   One page to each assessor's map
       d.   All of the above

15.   A Grantor Index are formatted
       a.   As one page per grantor
       b.   Alphabetically
       c.   Chronologically
       d.   All of the above

The Title Exam Review Questions

1.   What basic items does the title exam report?

2.   A chain of title is a compilation of what?

3.   Provide four obvious breaks in the chain of title you may encounter.

4.   Provide three common defects in title you might encounter during your search.

5.   Name four additional records you might refer to during your research beyond the basic indexes and maps.

6.   Fill in the recorded items the abstract must recite in chronological order.

7.   Provide two reasons that an abstract might contain faulty data without the responsibility being the abstractors.

8.   What protection does title insurance offer?

_____
_____
_____
_____
_____

9.   The chain is arranged _____ from the initial government patent or original source of the title to the present _____.

10.   The chain of title is complete when all events are _____ from the original source of title to the present owner. If there is a _____ link, the current owner does not have _____ title to the property.

11.   A chain of title is a record that links all previous lenders in order of priority.
    a.   True
    b.   False

12.   To research a chain of title you should all review
    a.   linkage of all owners from the original land grant to today
    b.   all matters or record that pertain to the property of research
    c.   any breaks in the chain of title that appear
    d.   all of the above

13.   In all cases, the chain of title will begin with the original government land grant to a company.
    a.   True
    b.   False

14.   Your search function will be contained only to those documents located within the recorder's office.
    a.   True
    b.   False

15.   A break in the chain of title may occur as a result of
    a.   a judicial determination not filed for record
    b.   insufficient deeds of conveyance
    c.   missing deeds or other documents
    d.   all of the above

16.   When a break in the chain of title exists, it should be
    a.   specifically excepted in the records
    b.   remedied through the proper procedures
    c.   noted and the next link in the chain researched
    d.   any of the above

17.   A defect in the title might be a result of the lack of termination of a
    a.   marriage
    b.   judgment
    c.   lien
    d.   any of the above

18.   Prior to considering an abstract complete, you must research
        a.   Local Tax Rolls
        b.   Lis Pendens Indexes
        c.   Mechanic's Liens
        d.   All of the above

19.   If a defect exists, your responsibility is to note the applicable data within your report so the underwriter may
        determine the handling of the defect.
        a.   True
        b.   False

20.   If a defect exists, you should
        a.   determine if the defect still exists and make the proper notation
        b.   detail any alterations that occurred with regard to the defect
        c.   note the method, time and processes that eliminated the defect
        d.   all of the above

21.   An abstract of title will include
        a.   a historical summary of the chain of title
        b.   the status of any defects that exist in the chain of title
        c.   a comprehensive explanation of any item of issue in the chain of title
        d.   all of the above

22.   The abstractor will
        a.   summarize each document located within the record
        b.   note the book and page of each document located within the record
        c.   note the date of each document entered into record
        d.   all of the above

23.   Individuals preparing the abstract are liable for mistakes they make during the research process.
        a.   True
        b.   False

24.   At times, mistakes in the preparation of the abstract may not be the fault of the abstractor conducting the search.

        a.   True
        b.   False

25.   Title insurance is designed to protect
        a.   issues that come to light after the completion of the abstract
        b.   the abstractor
        c.   the insurance holder
        d.   all of the above

Title Insurance Review Questions

1.   How does title insurance differ from other forms of insurance?

2.   What is a quiet title suit?

3.   What is a certificate of title?

4.   Name the four items that must be present for the issuance of title insurance.

5.   What are the components of a title insurance policy?

6.   What is the purpose of affirmative insurance?

7.   What is the major issue that arises with belated coverage causing additional scrutiny?

8.   The title commitment will be _____ with the same date and time that you noted as the
       _____ date and time for your abstracting summery

9.   Title commitment, commitment, or title binder refers to the _____ document _____ by the
       title company that provides formal contract to _____ the title.

10.   The _____ is the written declaration of a statement of _____ that is made
       voluntarily and sworn to or affirmed before some person legally _____ to administer an oath or
       affirmation.

11.   The title insurance process begins with
       a.   the title underwriter examining the file to determine suitability to the companies guidelines
       b.   the title attorney issuing an opinion as to the owner's rights to be transferred
       c.   the title abstractor examining public records to determine the status of the title
       d.   none of the above

12.   The title exam includes
       a.   a review of the chain of title
       b.   specifics of any defects encountered during research
       c.   information regarding the status of any defects encountered
       d.   all of the above

13.   Title insurance insures against future occurrences rather than past events
       a.   True
       b.   False

14.   The date and time you completed the abstract must be noted because
       a.   additional issues may arise following your abstract report
       b.   you must confirm the length of the search term
       c.   the insurance premiums will be based upon the time of your search
       d.   none of the above

15.   Title insurance issuance will be based on
       a.   the status of the purchaser
       b.   the completion of a search and exam of public records
       c.   the lender's assessment of borrower suitability
       d.   all of the above

16.   Schedule B of the title commitment will contain
       a.   the policies and commitment coverage's
       b.   the matters that affect the land as detailed in the legal description
       c.   general, standard, and special exceptions to coverage
       d.   all of the above

17.   When you discover a defect in the title insurance cannot be issued
       a.   True
       b.   False

18.   Affirmative insurance is also termed
       a.   positive insurance
       b.   insuring over
       c.   title insurance
       d.   none of the above

Overview Review Questions Answer Key

1. | Carefully and accurately, search public records | Review and establish a chain of title |
   | Determine any defects to the title that may exist | Document the status of these defects |

2. | The creation of the title commitment | The underwriting of specific issues on the property |
   | The issuance of title policies that contain title bulletins and exceptions | |

3. | A methodical approach to the tasks at hand | The ability to bring high levels of focus to your work |
   | Provide careful research | A dedication to the concise completion of each task |

4. Full-time employment with a title or closing company   Contract abstractor performing functions for various businesses

   Self-employed abstractor working to complete title search activities for individuals and businesses outside of the normal mortgage-lending sphere

5. The abstractor must determine how events that have occurred during the chain of title, often termed defects, effect the ability of the current owner of real property to transfer a full bundle of rights to the new purchaser

6. The date of the original land grant on the property through the last abstract certificate issued on that property

7. The abstractor will determine the rights and interests in the land and the ability of these rights to be transferred.

8. If the individual representing himself or herself as the owner of the property actually has the legal right to transfer the property in question

   What if any defects exist on the title of the property being researched including those defects brought against the current or past owner that directly impact the clarity of the title

9. Title companies insurance commitments

10. The career of real estate title abstractor is essential to the operation of the real estate title insurance and closing industries and as such requires careful, detail oriented, and methodical practices on your part.

11. D   12. D   13. C   14. D   15. B

Real Property Review Questions Answer Key

1. Surface rights, Sub-surface rights – including mineral rights, Air rights

2. | The intention of the parties in the transaction | An agreement between the parties in the transaction |
   | The manner in which the item is attached to the real property | The item itself and its adaptation to the real estate |

3. A built in appliance for which outside financing has been obtained using the appliance as security may not be insured as part of the lending process. This would be true although the fixture meets the four criteria unless the lien against the appliance is paid in full prior to the real property transfer. The appliance is still technically owned in part or in whole by the finance company.

4. to sever or remove a right or interest from the overall bundle of rights which will be transferred

5. Real property surface rights include the improvements that exist and area actually affixed to the surface of the land.

6. A fixture is a piece of personal property that has been affixed, installed or permanently attached to a parcel of land or the structures on the land.

7. Crops are also known as fructus industrias or fruits of industry.

8. A property's value is effected its ability to transfer full rights to the new purchaser.

9. Sub-surface resources are subject to the same rights of ownership as any other portion of the land.

10. If an item is classified as personal property, it will not be included in the sale of real property.

| 11. | D | 12. | A | 13. | B | 14. | A | 15. | C | 16. | A |
| 17. | D | 18. | A | 19. | A | 20. | A | | | | |

Land and Descriptions Review Questions Answer Key

1. Informal Reference   Metes and Bounds   Rectangular Survey   Recorded Plat
    Survey   State Referral Method   Referral to another document   Assessor's Parcel Number

2. INFORMAL REFERENCE   It is easily understood.

3. Degrees – 360 in a circle   Minutes – 60 minutes in a degree   Seconds – 60 seconds in minute

4. Point of beginning

5. Government Survey   US Public Land Survey

6. Rectangular Survey Method

7. 24 mile x 24 mile area

8. A survey is defined as the process of measuring land to determine its exact area.

9. The American Land Title Association   The American Congress of Surveying and Mapping

10. The metes and bounds method begins at a monument, which is a permanent reference mark.

11. Distance and direction is another term for metes and bounds surveying.

12. It is customary to describe a parcel by going clockwise.

13. Latitude lines run east-west while longitude lines run north-south.

14. Another term for the lot-block-tract system is the recorded plat.

15. The assessor's parcel number is a number assigned by the tax assessor to aid in tax collection.

| 16. | A | 17. | C | 18. | B | 19. | A | 20. | C |
| 21. | B | 22. | D | 23. | C | 24. | C | 25. | A |

Access and Rights Review Questions Answer Key

1. Be included in your abstract report with full details regarding the conveyance or condemnation of the access.

2. Physical access is: The actual ability to use an access point   Legal access is: The legal ability to use an access point

3. Consider every property landlocked until you have proven otherwise by finding conveyance of access that is undisputed.

4. The process by which a piece of land is increased or extended by the gradual deposit of soil as a result of the action of a river, stream, lake, pond or mass of tidal waters that border the property.

5. Whether the wet sand area is considered to be held by the government in trust

    Whether the title to the wet sand area is held for the benefit of the public

    Whether the public has acquired access to the use of any part of the beach area or access to the beach area through adverse use or local custom

6. A riparian right is a right that occurs when a property borders a river or stream.

7. A littoral right is a right that occurs when a property borders a sea OR lake.

9.   The <u>DOCTRINE</u> OF <u>prior appropriation</u> may come into effect that allows the first landowner that diverts water for his use to continue this diversion although it is not fair to other landowners.

10.   A common <u>appurtenance</u> would be an <u>easement</u> or right-of-way that was gained for that particular parcel of land.

11.	C	12.	D	13.	A	14.	A	15.	D
16.	A	17.	B	18.	B	19.	B	20.	B

Estates Review Questions Answer Key

1.   The government and the individual or entity owner

2.   An encumbrance is any claim, right, lien, estate or liability that limits the fee simple title to a property.

3.   Inheritance tax is paid when a decedent receives property at the time of the death of a grantor.

4.   Estate tax is the tax imposed on the right to transmit a piece of property upon death or in contemplation of death.

5.   The system of governing estates in the US most closely resembles the <u>Allodial</u> <u>system</u>.

6.   The highest and most complete form of estate ownership is the <u>freehold</u> <u>estate</u>, which is typically transferred using a <u>fee simple transfer</u>.

7.   A life estate provides a <u>lifelong right</u> to use and occupy and when it ends, the estate reverts to the original grantor who is also known as the <u>reversionary</u>.

8.   The concept of real estate ownership can be easiest understood when you view ownership as a <u>bundle of rights</u> or collection of rights to ownership.

9.   The abstract report is specifically concerned with rights that are <u>granted</u> as well as rights that are <u>limited</u> in a real estate transfer.

10.   If a person dies without a will or having disposed of their property, the laws of intestacy property will come into effect. This is also known as the <u>statutes of descent and distribution</u>.

11.	A	12.	C	13.	B	14.	D	15.	D	16.	B
17.	B	18.	B	19.	B	20.	D	21.	D	22.	B

Estate Limitations Review Questions Answer Key

1.   The level of interest one has in real property can be described as the collective rights of ownership interest in a property.

2.   Taxation   Eminent Domain   Police Power   Escheat

3.   Explain how a deed restriction or <u>reservation in deed</u> may be enforced. A deed restriction can be enforced through the civil courts through court action brought by any party who is affected by the restriction.

4.   The open, continuous, notorious and hostile use of the property of another for a proscribed period.

5.   The government right of <u>police power</u> is imposed to protect the health, <u>safety and general welfare</u> of the public.

6.   An example of government <u>easement by condemnation</u> occurs when the government is acting to control a flood area and runs a drainage pipe <u>over</u> or <u>under</u> an owner's property.

7.   The non-payment of <u>property taxes</u> may result in the government seizure of property resulting in the loss of an owner's interest. This occurs in an attempt to gain the needed revenue for specific operations.

8.   The process of <u>eminent domain</u> is the taking of a piece of private property for <u>public use</u>.

9.   If an individual loses the ability to enjoy full use of his property through the actions of another, he may bring an <u>inverse condemnation</u> suit.

10.   An easement grants the right to <u>come through</u> a certain portion of a privately owned property.

11.	B	12.	B	13.	A	14.	C	15.	D
16.	C	17.	B	18.	D	19.	A	20.	B

Forms of Ownership Review Questions Answer Key

1.   Ensure that you have a full understanding of all potential owners who may have obtained an interest to a piece of real property so that you may research any action each owner might have taken that has an impact on the title condition.

2.   Unity of Time   Unity of Title   Unity of Possession   Unity of Interest   Unity of Person

3.   Tenancy by the entirety   Joint tenancy   Tenancy in common

4.   Business Trusts   Credit Unions   Corporations   Aliens   Convicts
        Government Entities   Banks or Savings Institutions

5.   An individual   Married couples   Corporations considered a single entity

6.   Tenancy by Severalty is also known as <u>sole ownership</u> and means that the ownership of a property is CUT OFF FROM OTHER INDIVIDUALS AND THE NAMED INDIVIDUAL OWNS THE PROPERTY ALONE.

7.   Concurrent ownership is ownership held by <u>two</u> or more individuals.

8.   The term <u>guardianship</u> refers to the administration of the property and interest of a <u>minor</u> or <u>incompetent</u> individual.

9.   A title company may occasionally rely on either an <u>ante nuptial</u> or <u>prenuptial</u> agreement for the elimination of the marital rights of a spouse.

10.   Any action taken by <u>any</u> interested owner will affect the title to the <u>property</u> you are researching.

11.	C	12.	D	13.	D	14.	D	15.	D	16.	A

Liens and Encumbrances Review Questions Answer Key

1.   Voluntary lien created when a property owner voluntarily creates a lien against a property.

        Involuntary lien created by the operation or enforcement of the law.

2.   Declaratory Judgment   Money Judgment   Judgment in Rem   Federal Judgment
        Foreign Judgment   Dormant Judgment   Judgment in Personam

3.   A property is offered by the owner as security for the repayment of a mortgage debt.

4.   A legal procedure where the mortgagor or other lien holder obtains the real estate securing a debt that has fallen into default for the purpose of obtaining the funds owed on that debt.

5.   The first lien filed receives a higher priority than the later liens filed except those liens that usurp the priority of time.

6.   A <u>general lien</u> goes against an individual and attaches to all of the <u>real property</u> of that individual within the county.

7.   A <u>specific lien</u> goes against a specific property.

8.   The lien that always comes first in the order of priority regardless of the time is the <u>tax lien</u>.

9.   If you locate a judgment lien with regard to the property you are searching, you should research to determine if the judgment has been <u>terminated</u>.

10.   The <u>mechanic's lien law</u> gives anyone that has furnished <u>labor</u> or <u>materials</u> for the improvement of a parcel of land the right to place a lien against the improvements and the land.

11.	B	12.	B	13.	C	14.	B	15.	B	16.	D
17.	D	18.	B								

Deeds Review Questions Answer Key

1.   A deed conveys or transfers ownership interests in land from one person or entity to another.

2.   General Warranty Deed

3.   The seller who provides a grant-deed warrant only the time that particular owner had possession of the title.

4.   The bargain and sale deed contains no warranties and covenants. When using this type of deed the seller only implies that he owns the property described in the deed with no guarantee as to the condition of the title or the right to transfer the property.

5.   A correction deed is used to correct an error in a previously executed and delivered deed.

6.   Actual delivery

7.   Covenant against Encumbrances   Covenant of Seizin   Covenant of Enjoyment
     Covenant of Further Assurance   Covenant of Right to Convey   Covenant of Non-Claim

8.   An exception is included to withhold or exclude part of the estate or land being conveyed from the transfer.
9.   The basic bargain and sale deed contains no covenants and only the minimal essentials of the deed.

10. Each entry on the deed and the specific wording, inclusions and type of deed within the public records of the property you are researching will affect the rights of any future owner of that property.

11.	B	12.	D	13.	B	14.	C	15.	D	16.	A

Understanding Contracts Review Questions Answer Key

1.   All of the terms and conditions of the sale between a seller and a buyer.

2.   Offer to purchase   Option to buy or sell   Contract for the purchase of real estate
     Sales Agreement   Contract for deed

3.   Land Contract   Article of Agreement   Installment Land Contract

4.   The seller

5.   Possession of the property and equitable title

6.   Both parties may assign their interest in the property.

7.   An option to purchase real property is a contract that allows the right to purchase the property to a specific individual at a specific price and within a specific time frame.

8.   Establish that the option conveyed has expired in time.

     Establish that an additional document was created terminating the option.

     Generate the information that will be needed by the title underwriter to generate an exception regarding this option.

9.	B	10.	D	11.	A	12.	D	13.	A	14.	D
15.	D	16.	D								

Conducting the Search Review Questions Answer Key

1.   Through the recording of a document at the county recorder office.

Real Estate Title Search - Abstracting

2. Seen   Heard   Read   Observed   Witnessed

3. THE MOST RECENTLY RECORDED DOCUMENT AND WORK BACKWARD THROUGH THE RECORDS UNTIL YOU REACH THE ORIGINAL LAND GRANT.

4. A list of all recorded deeds, mortgages and other documents related to a particular parcel.

5. All grantors named in each document for a record year are listed in alphabetical order and placed in the grantor index.

6. A chain of title can be viewed as a group of links moving backward through time from the most recent transaction to the original land grant. If a link in the chain is broken or missing then the chain is not complete.

7. You will research all possible document storage locations to find the missing piece of information enabling you to mend the break in the chain. If the applicable information is not available, you will note all applicable details and refer the issue to the title underwriter assigned to the file.

8. Constructive notice is accomplished by the <u>recording</u> of a document at the county recorder office.

9. The simplest indexes to use are the <u>tract indexes</u>.

10. The documents presented for recording will be <u>photocopied</u> and the copies will be placed in the <u>book</u> with indexes.

    The book and index <u>pages</u> will be noted on the <u>document</u>.

11. D   12.   A   13.   D   14.   A   15.   D

The Title Exam Review Questions Answer Key

1. Chain of Title   Breaks in the Chain of Title   Defects in Title   Status of Defects

2. All real estate instruments and other matters of record that effect the title of a particular piece of land.

3. Missing deeds of conveyance
    Insufficient deeds of conveyance or other instruments
    Lack of adequate judicial proceedings
    Judicial determinations that are not filed for record at the office designated by statute
    Factual or non-judicial information that was not filed for record at the office designated by statute
    Other reasons as statutorily proscribed

4. Mortgages Liens   Judgments   Easements   Lawsuits   Active contracts

5. Birth records   Marriage records   Divorce records   Adoption records   Probate court records
    Military files   Federal tax lien logs   Assessment Record

6. Conveyances   Easements   Mortgages   Wills   Tax liens
    Agreements   Judgments   Pending lawsuits   Marriages   Divorces   Deaths

7. A married person represents himself on the deed, as a single person the deed may be invalidated.
    A minor might have executed the deed causing potential validity questions.
    An incompetent person may have executed the deed causing the validity of the deed to be called into question.
    The deed may contain erroneous descriptions.

8. Title insurance protects against losses that may arise from title defects that are not the fault of the abstractor and from title defects that were not located by the abstractor during the examination.

9. The chain is arranged <u>consecutively</u> from the initial government patent or original source of the title to the present <u>titleholder</u>.

10. The chain of title is complete when all events are <u>documented</u> from the original source of title to the present owner. If there is a <u>missing link</u>, the current owner does not have <u>valid</u> title to the property.

11. B   12.   D   13.   B   14.   B   15.   D
16. B   17.   D   18.   D   19.   A   20.   D

| 21. | D | 22. | D | 23. | A | 24. | B | 25. | D |

Title Insurance Review Questions Answer Key

1. Title insurance insures against occurrences that occurred from the date the covered individual secured the insurance into the past while typical insurance provides coverage against events that may occur in the future.

2. A quiet title suit is a court ordered hearing to determine land ownership.

3. A certificate of title is an opinion issued by an attorney detailing who rightfully owns a piece of land.

4. A complete search of public records   A valid title commitment
    A bona fide purchaser   Full disclosure of all matters that affect the property

5. Commitment   Schedules A and B   Affidavits
    Releases   Exceptions   Acknowledgments
    Endorsements   Validation of Acknowledgements

6. To insure over a specific defect lien, encumbrance or interest that affects the title.

7. The purchaser in possession of the property is not a bone fide purchaser. Any request at such a late time is suspect, causing one to consider that the owner may have gained knowledge of some defect he is now attempting to gain insurance coverage to offset.

8. The title commitment will be <u>dated</u> with the same date and time that you noted as the <u>completion</u> date and time for your abstracting summery

9. Title commitment, commitment, or title binder refers to the <u>binding</u> document <u>issued</u> by the title company that provides formal contract to <u>insure</u> the title.

10. The <u>affidavit</u> is the written declaration of a statement of <u>fact</u> that is made voluntarily and sworn to or affirmed before some person legally <u>authorized</u> to administer an oath or affirmation.

| 11. | C | 12. | D | 13. | B | 14. | A | 15. | B |
| 16. | C | 17. | B | 18. | C |

Real Estate Title Search - Abstracting

SAMPLE ABSTRACTOR SUMMARY

Date: _____ Client: _____

Search Purpose/Notes: _____

Property Street Address: _____

Map Book Number: _____ Map Parcel Number: _____ Taxes: $_____/_____Status: _____

Grantor: _____ Grantee: _____

Deed Book Volume: _____ Page Number: _____ Date: _____ Deed Type: _____

Legal Description: _____

_____

_____

Access: _____

Easements/Restrictions/Other Matters: _____

_____

Mortgage: _____ Satisfied: Y/N Book / Page: _____/_____ Borrower(s)

Name: _____

Notes: _____

Liens/Judgments/Other Matters: _____

Notes: _____

_____

_____

_____

_____

_____

_____

_____

_____

_____

_____

_____

_____

_____

The following quick list will assist you in locating the necessary records to complete the abstract of the title, locate any defects that exist and determine the status of any defects that exist within the chain of the title you are researching.

- **Grantee/Grantor Indexes**
  - ➢ Current Property Owner
    This entry will be located in the index for the year that the current owner obtained his interest in the property.

    The index will provide a reference to the book and page where the deed of conveyance by which he took title to the property is recorded.

  - ➢ Previous Owner
    A review of the deed of conveyance will provide you with the name of the owner from whom the current owner took possession. You will then work backward through the previous indexes to locate the entry that indicates the document by which this previous owner took ownership interest.

    By continuing this process backward through all deeds of conveyance, you will construct the chain of title.

- **Grantor / Grantee Index / Mortgagee Index**
  - ➢ Real property transfer documents
  - ➢ Liens
  - ➢ Judgments
  - ➢ Assignments
  - ➢ Power of attorney
  - ➢ Additional Contracts
  - ➢ Other matters pertaining to the specific title you are researching

  Some states will place mortgages within the general grantor and grantee indexes, while others will have ea separate index that details only mortgage instruments. You must determine the method employed in the state where you will conduct your research.

  If a mortgage is located within the public records, the applicable records will provide you with the status of the mortgage. The mortgage may be satisfied, release or active. If a mortgage is released and satisfied, the recorder's office will place a note on the margin of the recorded mortgage instrument indicating the book and page where the release is located.

- **Judgment Rolls, Lis Pendens Index, General Execution Docket**
  - ➢ General Liens
  - ➢ Specific Liens
  - ➢ Pending Lawsuits

  A defect on the title may exist in the form of a judgment or pending lawsuits may affect the transfer of ownership interest. You can locate information pertaining to judgments within the Judgment Rolls and relating to pending lawsuits within the Lis Pendens Index.

- **Assessor's Records / Ad Valorem Docket**
  - ➢ Current property taxes
  - ➢ Delinquent Taxes
  - ➢ Special Assessments
  - ➢ Tax Liens
  - ➢ Current owner name and address

- **County map records, survey reports and plat maps**
  - ➤ Legal Description
  - ➤ Property size
  - ➤ Boundary specifics
  - ➤ Boundary Line Issues or Agreements
  - ➤ Appurtenances
  - ➤ Easements
  - ➤ Right of Ways
  - ➤ Right of Access
  - ➤ Quality of Access
  - ➤ Abutting or adjoining property and roads
  - ➤ Measurements
  - ➤ Improvements
  - ➤ Easements
  - ➤ Utilities
  - ➤ Features
  - ➤ Accretion or Erosion that alters the land description
  - ➤ Littoral, riparian, beach rights
  - ➤ Flood Plain Designation

- **Tract Index**
  - ➤ Real property transfer documents
  - ➤ Liens
  - ➤ Judgments
  - ➤ Assignments
  - ➤ Power of attorney
  - ➤ Additional Contracts
  - ➤ Other matters pertaining to the specific title you are researching

- **Civil court records**
  - ➤ Foreclosure actions
  - ➤ Legal Proceedings against a property owner
  - ➤ Other legal proceedings

- **Divorce Records**
  - ➤ To locate the removal of a property owner's interest through a divorce decree

- **Marriage Records**
  - ➤ To determine the addition of a potential property owner through a marriage

- **Probate court records**
  - ➤ Additional interest transfers
  - ➤ Status of inheritance and estate tax payments

- **State and Federal tax lien logs**
  To aid in the determination of whether any federal or state liens against a property owner may have attached to the property

Appendix C Glossary of Terms

Abstractor: individual who specializes in research relevant to the chain of title

Abut: touch

Accretion: the build-up of soil caused by the action of water or wind

Accrue: to increase or accumulate. Mortgage interest is said to accrue daily

Actual Notice: personal knowledge of an interest or instrument

Addendum: an attachment to a purchase agreement or to escrow instructions that alters or negotiates the transaction specifics

Ad Valorem: a Latin term that means 'according to value' Taxes are sometimes assessed on an ad valorem basis

Adverse Possession: obtaining title from another by the open, hostile, continuous use of property for a specific period set forth by statute

Affidavit: a statement sworn under oath or before a notary

Affirmation: a formal declaration regarding the truthfulness of a statement

Affirmative Easement: a type of easement that allows the easement holder the right to use the land of another landowner

Agreement of Sale: the real estate purchase contract

Air Rights: the rights to the use of the airspace located above a piece of property

Alienation Clause: a clause that calls an entire loan balance due and payable. This is also termed an acceleration clause or due on sale clause

Allodial System: a system of land ownership where the ownership is held by individuals rather than the government. The US follows this system of ownership

Alluvion: the gradual addition of soil to a property by the action of water

Amortization: The method by which a loan is paid down with each subsequent payment

Annual Percentage Rate: the yearly rate of interest on a loan

Ante nuptial Agreement: an agreement executed between a man and a woman prior to marriage to resolve and settle future issues

Appropriation Process: The enactment of a taxing authority's budget and money sources into legally required payment.

Appurtenance: rights, benefits, and attachments that transfer with real property

Appurtenant Easement: an easement that transfers with the land

Arrears: term used when describing a past due payment

ARM: adjustable rate mortgage

Assessed Value: the value placed on a property by the county assessor

Assessor's Map: The map that shows the assessor's parcel number for all land parcels within a specific taxing area

Assignment: the transfer, in writing, of one's interest in something

Assumption: the taking over of another person's financial obligation

Balloon Payment: the final payment that pays a note in full

Bankruptcy: a legal procedure that eliminates unsecured debt or relinquishes property to eliminate secured debt

Bargain and Sale Deed: a deed that uses the term bargain and sale and contains no warranties other than implied interest on the part of the seller

Base Line: Latitude line that acts as a reference in the rectangular survey system

Bilateral Escrow Instructions: a set of escrow instructions signed by both the buyer and the seller

Binder: insurance coverage given by an agent prior to the issuance of the full insurance policy

Cession Deed: deed that conveys all rights of an individual in real property to a county or municipality

Chain of Title: the history, in chronological order, of a property from the original government grant to the present owner

Close of Escrow: the date when the documents are recorded and title passes from the seller to the buyer

Closing Costs: the costs that are payable to close escrow not including the purchase price of a property

Collateral: real or personal property pledged as security for a loan

Competent: legally qualified to conduct transactions

Concurrent Escrow: a procedure where the one closing is dependent on the completion of another closing. Also termed a double escrow

Condemnation: the legal action to take a property for public use by eminent domain

Consideration: the amount of money or services given in exchange for the transfer of a property

Constructive Notice: the notice given by occupancy or recording of an interest in real property

Contingency: a condition that must be met or event that must happen before a contract will be considered binding

Convey: the transfer of title from one person to another

Covenant: a written agreement as to the use of a property

Declaration of Restriction: declaration of the restrictions contained in a deed of conveyance

Deed: a document that conveys interest and title to real property

Deed in Lieu of Foreclosure: a deed from a property owner to a lien holder made to avoid full foreclosure proceedings.

Deemer Period: the method that the state regulates the rate of filing by the title company

Deficiency Judgment: a judgment obtained when the foreclosure sale does not satisfy a debt in full

Descent: the hereditary succession by law when a property owner dies without a valid will

Determinable Fee Estate: an estate that would end on the occurrence of a specific event

Dominant Estate: an estate for which an easement is granted

Disbursement: the release of funds held in an escrow account

Earnest Money: a deposit by a buyer to a seller to bind an agreement

Easement by Necessity: an easement granted out of a valid need for the easement

Easement by Prescription: an easement created by the open, continuous, hostile, and notorious use of the property of another for a specified period of time

Easement in Gross: a personal easement to use the land of another in which no dominant estate exists

Emblements: cultivated crops that are considered personal property

Eminent Domain: the government's right to take private property for public use with just compensation paid to the property owner for the loss

Encroachment: the unauthorized intrusion on, over, or under the land of another

Escrow: the act of depositing papers and or money with an impartial third party until a transaction is complete

Escrow Instructions: a series of instructions from a buyer, seller, lender, or other interested party as to the acts that must be completed and conditions that must be met prior to the transfer of a property

Equitable Title: title obtained during the period between the creation of an agreement or contract and the finalization of a transaction

Escheat: the reversion of a property to the state when a person dies without a valid will and no heirs as identified by statute

Exception in Deed: exclusion in a deed that deeds only one portion of a property

Fee Simple Estate: the highest level of ownership possible the fee simple ownership includes the full bundle of rights

Fee Simple Determinable: a grant that ends if a property is no longer used for a designated purpose

Fee Tail Estate: an estate that limits conveyance to the heirs and decedents of the owner

Fixture: an item of personal property that is permanently attached to real property in a manner that causes it to become real property

Foreclosure: a legal process that deprives an owner of his or her rights to a property

Funding: the release of loan money from a lender to the escrow company

General Warranty Deed: a deed where the grantor warrants title against the claims of all others

Gift Deed: a deed that transfers real property for love and affection rather than valuable consideration

Good Consideration: love and affection are considered good consideration

Grant: the act of conveying title to a property

Grantee: the person who receives a deed, grant, or other item

Granting Clause: a deed provision showing that title is passing

Grantor: the person giving or conveying the deed, grant, or other item

Grantor/Grantee Index: an index system for researching chain of title that lists grantor/grantee names

Guardianship: the administration of the property of a minor or incompetent person

Habendum: a to have and to hold clause indicating the extent of the ownership being transferred

Impound: to accumulate borrower funds to meet the periodic payments due under tax billings or insurance billings

Improvement: an addition to land that is considered real property

Indemnity: a guarantee against loss

Incompetent: a person who is deemed incapable of making a legal decision or entering a legal contract due to age or mental capacity

Informal Reference: a description of property that uses items such as number, street, or address. This is not a legal description of property

Instrument: a written legal document such as a sales agreement, contract, or promissory note

Inverse Condemnation: an action instituted by a property owner forcing the government to take property where the property use is restricted by an action taken by the government or other public entity

Involuntary Lien: a lien imposed without the consent of a property owner

Joint Tenancy: an undivided interest that contains all unities except the unity of person

Judgment in Personam: a judgment against a person. When recorded the judgment becomes a specific lien against a particular property of the person involved in the action

Judgment in Rem: a judgment against specific property. When recorded the judgment becomes a specific lien against the property involved in the action

Judicial Foreclosure: a foreclosure that requires court proceedings for finalization

Jurat: the statement or certificate of the individual witnessing signatures to specific instruments

Legal Access: the legal right to use a specified access point

Legal Description: a description of real property that can be considered legally binding

Lender Instructions: the instructions received from a lender stating the requirements that must be met before a transaction can be closed

Lien: a monetary encumbrance secured by real property

Life Estate: an estate that exists for the lifetime of a specific person

Lis Pendens: pending lawsuit

Littoral rights: the rights of a property owner to the use of a lake, pond, or ocean water that borders his or her property in a reasonable manner

Mechanic's Lien: a specific lien against real property placed by a contractor for work performed to the property or property improvements when the charges are not paid as agreed by the property owner

Meridians: north-south lines used by government surveyors for measuring and describing real property

Metes and Bounds: a method of legal description by measurement and boundary of real property

Monument: a fixed marker used in surveys within the metes and bounds method

Mutual Consent: approval of both parties regarding the terms of a contract

Negotiable: able to be assigned or transferred

Notary Public: the person enabled by the property authorities to witness signatures, oaths or other matters

Offset Statement: the statement by an owner or lien holder detailing the liens against a piece of property

Option: a right given by the owner of property to another to buy a property at an agreed upon price and within an agreed upon time

Personal Property: property that is not classified as real property

Physical Access: access is the actual ability to use an access point

Police Power: the power of the state to enforce laws to promote the health and safety of the general public through the taking of a privately held piece of land

Post-nuptial Agreement: an agreement executed between a husband and wife following marriage to determine and settle specific issues

Prescription: an easement obtained by the open, hostile, continuous and notorious use of another's property for a regulated period of time

Prior Appropriation: a theory used in some states that allows the first user to divert water to maintain that sole interest in the water even though the use may not be equitable to other landowners

Priority: taking place in order or precedence over. In a real estate transaction, priority is typically established by the date of the recording of an instrument or specific wording within an instrument. The government right of taxation may usurp priority

Proration: the method employed to divide taxes, interest, and other sums between a buyer and a seller based upon a certain date

Quiet Enjoyment: the right of an owner to use their property without interference

Quitclaim Deed: a deed conveying whatever interest a grantor holds in real property. This type of deed makes no claim to actual ownership

Real Property: land and all that goes with the land

Recordation: the act of recording valid documents with the office of record to serve notice to all regarding the instruments recorded

Redemption: the act of reclaiming the title to property from someone who has taken legal interest in it

Redemption Period: the time in which an individual may redeem the interest in his or her property

Release: the relinquishment or giving up of a specific right or claim of interest

Remainder Interest: an interest obtained by a third party after the expiration of a life estate

Reservation: a specific right withheld by the grantor when conveying property

Restrictive Covenant: a restriction where the owner is limited as to the use of his or her property

Reversionary Interest: an interest to a property by the original grantor following the occurrence of a specific event

Right of Way: the right to pass over the land of another

Riparian Rights: rights of a landowner to use flowing water located on, under or adjacent to his or her property in a reasonable manner

Security: the property pledged to secure the repayment of a loan

Servient Estate: an estate that bears the burden of an easement

Sheriff's Deed: a deed given by a sheriff when a property is sold for the execution of a judgment or at foreclosure sale

Special Warranty Deed: a deed where the seller warrants the title only against defects occurring during his or her ownership

Statute of Limitations: the time limit within which legal proceedings may be implemented and action brought

Subject To: to take title without paying off one or more existing liens or notes

Sub-surface Rights: the right to the space and natural resources contained below the surface of a particular parcel of land

Surface Rights: the right to use the surface of a parcel of land. Commonly known as the rights to the land and the improvements of the land

Survey: a verification of property lines or the creation of a legal description created by a surveyor

Survivorship: the right of a joint tenant to obtain the interest of another tenant upon the death of the other party or other event that negates the interest of the other party

Tax Deed: a deed obtained as a result of a tax sale

Tenancy: method of holding ownership or interest in a property

Tenancy by the Entirety: a form of joint tenancy held by husband and wife and containing all of the forms of unity

Title: ownership Title is passed by deed

Vest: to convey or confer

Vesting: the manner in which title to real property is held. Method of interest in real property

Void: having no legal effect

Voidable: capable of being voided or valid only until voided

Voluntary Lien: a lien created by the action of the property owner in consideration of money borrowed

Waiver: the release of a right

www.ingramcontent.com/pod-product-compliance
Lightning Source LLC
Chambersburg PA
CBHW081434270326
41932CB00019B/3202